I0057094

Employee Ownership

EMPLOYEE SHARE OWNERSHIP PLANS

A NEW BUSINESS MODEL TO ATTRACT, RETAIN, AND REWARD YOUR KEY PEOPLE TO HELP YOU BUILD A SIGNIFICANT BUSINESS.

Dr Craig West

Dr Craig West

Succession Plus Pty Ltd
Level 10, 60 Castlereagh St
SYDNEY NSW 2000
www.succession.plus

©Craig West 2024

National Library of Australia Cataloguing-in-Publication data:
West, Craig, 1968-. Employee Ownership
ISBN 978-0-9922939-6-3

1. Employee Ownership
2. Employee Share Ownership Plans
3. Peak Performance Trust
4. Succession Planning
5. Exit Planning

I. Title.

658.3142

All rights reserved. No part of this publication may be reproduced, stored in a retrieval system, or transmitted in any form or by any means, electronic, mechanical, photocopying, recording or otherwise, without the publisher's prior permission.

Disclaimer

The material in this publication is of the nature of general comment only and neither purports nor intends to be advice. Readers should not act based on any matter in this publication without considering (and, if appropriate, taking) professional advice with due regard to their circumstances. The author and publisher expressly disclaim all and any liability to any person, whether a purchaser of this publication or not, in respect of anything and of the consequences of anything done or omitted to be done by any such person in reliance, whether whole or partial, upon the whole or any part of the contents of this publication.

CONTENTS

INTRODUCTION

I have been a strategic accountant and adviser to small businesses for over 25 years. Throughout that time, I have identified several key steps business owners can take to improve their financial performance dramatically.

One of these is having an employee incentive program that motivates staff to think and act less like employees and more like business owners. The ability to attract, retain, and inspire people to peak performance means attracting and retaining business – a significant competitive advantage. It can mean the difference between success and failure.

Until now, the most attractive employee incentive systems have been created to meet the needs of large corporates rather than smaller companies. In this book, we highlight the Peak Performance Trust (PPT). This employee equity plan has been created to give privately owned companies access to the same sophisticated incentive benefits that large companies use. The PPT enables you to create a structure within which your employees' lifestyle and financial goals are aligned with your business objectives. The result? A cohesive and committed team that is single-minded about working toward and sharing the benefits of a successful and profitable business.

This book is broken up into three parts:

- Part 1 - gives you an overview of the critical issues in implementing a Peak Performance Trust (PPT) within your company. It is a general discussion for business owners who want an overview of ESOPs and, in particular, PPTs.
- Part 2 - provides more technical explanation for both business owners and their advisers on how ESOPs work.

- Part 3 - showcases case studies of businesses that have successfully implemented ESOPs, providing real-world examples of how they can be used as effective business succession and exit planning tools.

When you are ready to talk about how a PPT can benefit your company's growth and profitability, you will have a good understanding of the requirements and scope of the process. So please enjoy this short read, and then let's talk about your peak performance needs.

Dr Craig West
Founder & Chairman
Succession Plus

For more worksheets, articles, advice, and information on employee incentive schemes, visit www.succession.plus or call our team on 1300 665 473.

PART 1

OVERVIEW OF EMPLOYEE OWNERSHIP

Is this the competitive edge you've been looking for?

"Managers thinking like owners is my dream."

Warren Buffett

Staff recruitment, satisfaction, motivation, and retention are often dismissed as part of the 'soft' skill set, which is less important than the real business of generating revenues and earning profits. But ask any small or medium-sized business owner what their greatest challenge yet most valuable asset is, and all will agree – it's their staff. What would it mean to your business if your employees were as committed to achieving success as you are?

Recent surveys confirm what most owners of small and medium-sized businesses know only too well – their number one concern, above even cash flow problems or a lack of sales, is finding and keeping the best people. In an employment market experiencing the impacts of an ageing workforce, skills shortages and a new generation of more mobile, demanding, and less loyal employees, employee retention is becoming one of today's hottest competitive issues.

Not investing in your employees is too expensive.

Employee turnover can represent significant costs to businesses in terms of:

- recruitment and training
- disruption to the team dynamic
- disruption to relationships with customers, suppliers and other third parties
- disruption to business continuity
- and a variety of other direct and indirect costs.

One estimate suggests that businesses lose at least two months of productive time through recruitment, training, loss of momentum and other factors when a staff member leaves. It costs about 45% of a person's annual salary in direct costs to replace someone (recruitment, training, onboarding, etc.). This doesn't include the cost of the intellectual property and business knowledge that has just walked out the door. Simply, losing staff means replacement costs, foregone opportunities and even increased competition if that's who is recruiting your best performers.

According to several recent studies, one of the critical issues for business owners is the ability to attract and recruit employees:

1. **Contextualizing Employment Outcomes in Family Business Research** (2021): This study reviews 67 articles on employment-related outcomes in family businesses, including recruitment, growth, downsizing, and quality of labour.
2. **Human Resource Management in Family Firms** (2021): This review integrates research on various HR topics in family firms, including recruitment and selection.
3. **Family Business Succession and Innovation** (2023): While primarily focused on succession and innovation, this study also touches on recruitment challenges during succession processes.

Employee incentive schemes as a strategic business tool

Recruiting staff is an expensive, time-consuming, and often hazardous process. In a job market where the best candidates are often interviewing you rather than the other way around, businesses need to find ways of differentiating themselves through innovative and attractive terms of employment.

Specific strategies to attract, motivate and retain employees can deliver valuable payoffs. Employee incentive schemes that get your people thinking and acting less like employees and more like business owners are essential tools. Their primary objective (and the reason for their success) is to align your employees' financial objectives with your business–which translates into a significant competitive advantage.

Recent research continues to highlight the positive impact of Employee Share Ownership Plans (ESOPs) on enterprise performance and worker productivity. Here are some key findings:

1. **Performance Improvement**: A significant study by Douglas Kruse and Joseph Blasi from Rutgers University found that ESOPs in closely held companies increase sales, employment, and sales per employee by about 2.3% to 2.4% per year compared to companies without ESOPs.
2. **Resilience During Crises**: Research from Rutgers University also showed that companies with ESOPs had higher sales growth during and after the 2008-2009 financial crisis and outperformed non-ESOP companies during the COVID-19 pandemic in terms of job retention, pay, benefits, and workplace health and safety.

3. **Employee Benefits and Job Quality**: ESOPs are associated with better job quality and employee wealth-building opportunities. Employees in ESOP companies report higher wages, better benefits, and greater job security than non-ESOP employees.

These findings suggest that ESOPs enhance enterprise performance and contribute to a more engaged and productive workforce.

A principal-agent behavioural theory argues that employee logical self-interest, aversion to risk and effort, create costs for an organisation. In the absence of complete information, the principal (business owner) must increase productivity through a mixture of compensation and monitoring of agents (employees). ESOPs are a way to align the principal and agents' efforts to improve productivity.

They have also been argued to reduce wealth inequality and improve firm and aggregate economic outcomes (Kozlowski, 2013). Policymakers and advocates also consider ESOPs an important mechanism to encourage Start-up activity by enabling employers to improve cash flows and attract and retain talented staff at lower wage compensation rates, when supplemented with shares or options (Department of Prime Minister and Cabinet, 2014).

This is all evident in Computershare's Employee Share Plan Survey in 2020, which found:

- Plan participants stay longer with the company and work longer hours
- Participants take less unplanned absence
- Participants are less likely to leave the company
- Participants are more motivated and more loyal
- 52% of participants said that the plan reduced the chance that they would leave the company either 'to a great extent' or 'to some extent', compared with 25% of non-participants
- 55% of plan participants say that the plan motivates them to some or a great extent; while the benefits are also extended to those who don't join. 27% of non-participants also say they are motivated by the plan
- 69% of participants feel very loyal to the company, compared to 63% of non-participants

Why do workers get into an ESOP?

In a Melbourne University study, a group of employees were asked specific questions and below are what they ranked as the most important elements of an ESOP:

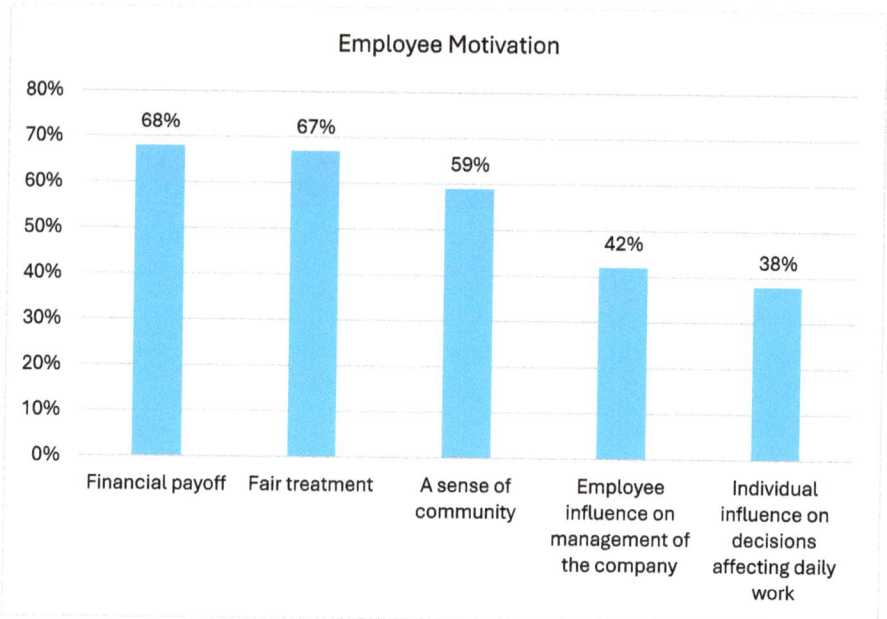

Employee Motivation

Category	Percentage
Financial payoff	68%
Fair treatment	67%
A sense of community	59%
Employee influence on management of the company	42%
Individual influence on decisions affecting daily work	38%

Source: Michelle Brown, Rowan Minson, Ann O'Connell and Ian Ramsay, Why Do Employees Participate in Employee Share Ownership Plans? Employee Share Ownership Project, Melbourne Law School, The University of Melbourne, 2011

ESOPS are used for several reasons:

- **Savings Vehicle** – Most ESOP plans have a long-term focus (between 5 and 20 years), allowing employees to accumulate savings by acquiring and holding shares.
- **Participation** – ESOP participants tend to experience a greater sense of community and involvement with the decision-making process, leading to increases in employee engagement levels.
- **Exit Planning** – An ESOP can be an effective employee buy-out instrument when the owner(s) want to retire (or change their business direction) and need to sell.
- **Succession Planning** – An ESOP can also be used as part of a succession strategy where the owners (family) want majority ownership but must incentivise a key group of managers to align their interests.
- **Funding Retirement** - ESOPs can allow founders to extract cash before retirement.

Academic Research on the Impact of ESOPs

1. **Employee Retention and Retirement Savings**: A 2023 National Center for Employee Ownership (NCEO) study found that ESOPs significantly reduce voluntary quit rates and increase retirement savings. Employees at S Corporation had more than double the retirement savings compared to their non-ESOP counterparts.

2. **Performance During Economic Downturns**: Research from 2022 highlighted that ESOP companies in the food industry fared better during the COVID-19 pandemic in terms of workforce retention, benefits, and firm performance. ESOP companies had lower involuntary separation rates and were more likely to offer employer-paid healthcare.

3. **Firm Performance and Growth**: Studies have shown that ESOP firms have higher sales growth and sales per worker than non-ESOP firms. For instance, a study examining 300 privately held companies that set up ESOPs between 1988 and 1994 found significantly higher sales growth in ESOP firms.

4. **Employment Stability and Survival**: ESOP companies are linked to greater employment stability and are less likely to go bankrupt or close

than non-ESOP firms. A study tracking ESOP companies over ten years found that privately held ESOPs were only half as likely to go bankrupt or close as non-ESOP firms.

5. **Global Reach of ESOPs**: A 2024 study by Rutgers University, commissioned by the Employee-Owned S Corporations of America (ESCA), found that multinational ESOP-owned companies gain competitive advantages in international markets. These companies reported benefits such as increased employee productivity, recruitment and retention, corporate reputation, and customer loyalty.

While the research undoubtedly shows an increase in employees looking for equity in the business they work for, Australia needs to catch up and provide a mechanism to achieve this. According to recent research in the United States and Europe, a little over 30% of employees have some equity interest in the business they work for, whilst in Australia, that number is around 8%. Of the estimated $8 trillion of corporate equity in the United States, employees own about $213 billion through ESOPs and similar stock plans, with over 10 million participants in over 6,400 corporations.

In Australia, one of the main reasons for this low participation rate is that many businesses don't realise that share ownership is appropriate for them, even though it can be used in any business – even those not publicly listed on an exchange. There are various options and several different types of plans that can be used to allow employees to own equity in the business they work for.

ESOPs and Gen Y

A workshop on Generation Y in the workplace raised an interesting statistic: 72% of the Generation Y population wants to own their own business. Back in my dad's generation, less than 12% of school leavers wanted to run their own business – most people wanted to go and work for a big bank or a corporation and stay there until they were 65, then retire on a good retirement plan.

If you have Generation Y employees, this is an important point, as they may leave to pursue their goals if equity ownership is not an option. However, another interesting statistic was that over 90% of those wanting to own a business said they didn't want to own it on their own. Generation Y workers look for freedom and flexibility and the opportunity to have three months off to travel to Europe.

Most baby boomers look at that and think it's all too hard, they get it too easy, or they are too risky. But the fact is that this is the way our workforce is heading, and rather than fight it, we need to look for ways to accommodate it so that we can retain good people.

Most 25-year-olds can't afford to start or buy their own business. So, an employee share plan allows younger employees to own at least part of a business while enjoying the security and lifestyle that comes with being an employee. Over the next five to ten years, that employee can build equity and gradually take ownership of the business if they want it.

A strategic approach to remuneration

"Research indicates that workers have three prime needs: interesting work, recognition for doing a good job, and being let in on things that are going on in the company."

Zig Ziglar

Far from just paying people a standard wage or salary and providing the minimum mandatory benefits (such as company-funded superannuation and basic leave entitlements), your remuneration strategy should help you to attract the best people, to get the best performance from them once they're on the job and encourage them to stay with you for the long term.

A strategically planned remuneration system can be a powerful tool for engaging your employees in your business's performance and rewarding them for their contribution to its success. It should:

- **Offer a tangible incentive to employees to perform (achieve targets).**
- **Enable people to share in the value they create for the organisation.**
- **Assist employees in achieving their own financial and lifestyle objectives.**
- **Align employee performance (behaviour) with company strategic goals.**

The way you pay your employees affects their behaviour

Transforming employees into committed stakeholders in your business means developing a remuneration system that reflects your organisation's philosophy, objectives and values. Many small and medium-sized businesses don't fully appreciate how remuneration practices influence their staff's thinking, behaviour, and performance.

How companies pay their employees communicates their values and contributes enormously to their culture, the type of people they attract, and the results they deliver. So, a remuneration strategy must be developed with the organisation's objectives in mind.

Consider the example of a business that only pays its people a standard wage for a standard working day – what is that company saying to its employees? It is saying that 9 am to 5 pm thinking is all that is required and that anything outside of that should come at an extra cost to the company in the form of overtime payments. Do you think that these staff are staying back late or coming in early to get the job done? Or are they giving their job a moment's thought outside their standard workday?

16

What about a company that pays bonuses or commissions to individuals for monthly or quarterly results? This communicates the message that it's everyone for him or herself, which encourages a fiercely independent and even competitive organisational culture. The frequency of bonus payments tells employees what timeframe they should be focused on, which can be a valuable tool in encouraging specific short-term results. However, without the additional ability to focus people's attention on the longer term, the message is that all they need to be focused on is the next bonus or commission timeframe. In this case, you may start to see 'sales-bulking', when staff hold and roll over sales from one bonus period into the next, rather than doing more than is necessary to earn a bonus in the current period.

If a company's incentives are only based on sales, then that's what its employees focus on – sometimes at the expense of margin. Their focus would differ if rewards were based on maximising gross margin dollars rather than just gross revenue.

And what if a company places an upper limit on the amount of bonus or commission that can be earned? Do you think its employees will continue to drive for results beyond the maximum amount they will be rewarded?

How companies pay people determines how they think and behave, which impacts the bottom line.

Why a pay packet is not enough

Employee remuneration is more than just money – it is about motivation and reward. Remuneration comprising economic and non-economic benefits will contribute toward increased productivity and morale. One of the most powerful outcomes of a strategically planned remuneration system is that it helps to align your employees' personal and financial goals with your business goals; in other words, it encourages employees to think and act like owners in your business.

The ideal mix would include base remuneration, short-term performance bonuses and long-term loyalty bonuses to achieve this.

Base Pay and Compulsory Employee Benefits

This must be industry competitive. If you pay less than the rest of the market, you will attract a lower-quality employee, which will be reflected in your operating results. Compulsory employee benefits such as superannuation, annual leave, personal leave and so on can also be enhanced to help position your company as an employer of choice and will help you retain high-performing staff. For example, company-funded superannuation contributions could be increased after several years of service, or additional paid annual leave could be offered to long-standing employees. Many businesses offer well-being or "me" days – additional leave every month; others provide five-hour workdays or four-day working weeks.

Discretionary Employee Benefits

These may be financial (such as bonus payments, employer-funded health insurance or study leave) or non-financial.

Non-financial incentives recognise and reward performance and demonstrate a commitment to employees by assisting them in achieving some of their lifestyle objectives.

Short-term non-financial incentives might include tickets to the theatre or a sporting event, dinner at a restaurant, a weekend away, a pat on the back or public acknowledgment for a job well done. They may be awarded to individuals or to teams to enjoy together.

Long-term non-financial incentives include flexible working hours, the option to work from home, the provision of childcare facilities, job sharing and so on.

Examples of Discretionary Employee Benefits

- generous long service leave provisions
- shopping vouchers
- family dinners, movies or holidays
- one-off thank-you gifts
- office lunches
- afternoons off
- contributions to nominated charities
- birthday gift vouchers
- reimbursement of study fees
- study leave or flexible hours for study
- payment of children's school fees
- funded health insurance
- additional superannuation contributions
- flexible hours
- work from home
- dry-cleaning pick up and drop off at the office
- childcare facilities
- dependent care days
- job sharing
- commuting assistance
- casual dress days
- health promotion programs
- reimbursement of gym fees
- club memberships
- personal legal, accounting and financial planning services.

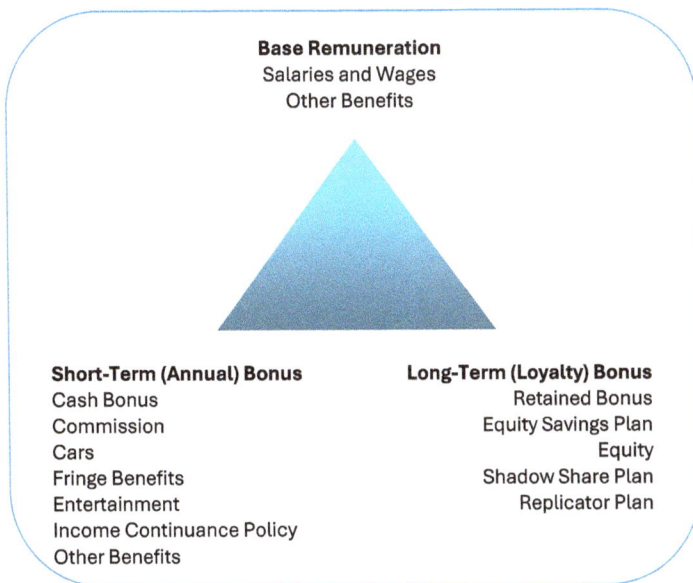

Base Remuneration
Salaries and Wages
Other Benefits

Short-Term (Annual) Bonus
Cash Bonus
Commission
Cars
Fringe Benefits
Entertainment
Income Continuance Policy
Other Benefits

Long-Term (Loyalty) Bonus
Retained Bonus
Equity Savings Plan
Equity
Shadow Share Plan
Replicator Plan

Successful remuneration strategies attract and retain employees by rewarding high performance over both the short and long term.

Performance-Based Pay

This is about rewarding people for their results and should include short-term and long-term incentives.

Short-term incentives are designed to influence immediate behaviour to achieve specific short-term goals. They might take the form of cash bonuses, commissions, fringe benefits or anything meaningful to the employee but that does not cost the company unnecessarily in terms of margin.

Long-term incentives provide employees with a vested interest in increasing the organisation's value. In the US and UK, long-term incentives can make up between 50 and 60 per cent of an executive's annual remuneration. There is a growing global trend toward decreasing the percentage of fixed remuneration and increasing the percentage of remuneration at risk in both the short and long term. With high-performing staff, linking higher remuneration to results is a win/win for both the business and the employee – the sky is the limit. Many long-term incentive schemes include a vesting period, often up to five years, which means that the employee must remain with the company for a longer period before they can enjoy the full benefits of the scheme.

Employee incentive scheme tips and traps

As much as they can offer significant benefits to employers and employees alike, remuneration systems that are not adequately developed or implemented can also be a disincentive. At their most ineffective, such systems can cause a loss of trust, engagement, or faith in the organisation. You can avoid messing up your system by working with expert advisers and following these simple rules.

Effective remuneration systems use SMARTS:

Simple
The system must be well thought out and easy for staff to understand so that they know how it applies to them.

Applicable
While the levels of remuneration and reward may differ, the process should apply consistently to all employees.

Employees should only benefit from a positive outcome over which they have had some input, and they should not be penalised for a negative outcome over which they had no influence.

Reliable
Once the system is established and communicated to staff, avoid making unnecessary or frequent changes.

Transparent
The system should be communicated in plain English, and relevant information should be disclosed regularly in a format easily understood by all staff.
All performance indicators must be measured objectively, preferably using systems and data, particularly where a subjective performance appraisal is a factor in determining an employee's eligibility for a performance bonus.

Once launched, the company's owners and managers must fully support the system.

While financial and lifestyle goals are critical motivators for people, most are also substantially driven by intrinsic rewards: job satisfaction, the opportunity to rise and meet new challenges, and recognition for a job well done. So, while generous remuneration and employee incentive schemes are essential, they're just one component of an integrated and satisfying work experience that will help your organisation retain the best people over the long term.

Other important aspects of staff retention include:

- creating a positive and supportive work environment
- recognising and catering to individual differences
- matching the right people with the right jobs
- using realistic and achievable goals and targets to challenge people
- implementing training and programs for professional development and career advancement.

Ladder to Equity

While the research undoubtedly shows an increase in employees looking for equity in the business they work for, Australia needs to catch up and provide a mechanism to achieve this.

The issue is a simple mechanism to manage the transition through various stages. It is not simple or wise to take an employee and provide them with equity; thus, the ladder becomes essential.

As Warren Buffet says -

"Employees are keen to climb the ladder to equity – but someone needs to provide the ladder."

Progressive staged approach:

Employee Earnings > Income Model > Profit Share > Equity > Control

- Employee Earnings – Earning (salary/wage/hourly rates, etc.) is where most employees start (and stay).

- Income Model – The first step on the ladder is to boost income, which is quite common. We often see companies paying bonuses, commissions on sales, incentives, etc., to increase an employee's income. This is an excellent step in linking performance with reward. However, these must be designed very carefully to avoid negative behaviours.

- Profit Share – Most equity plans include this simple step, and many end at this step. Simply providing a share of profits to employees is a tremendous additional incentive, as they are directly rewarded for the company's financial performance like a business owner typically would be. This step changes the focus from personal to team performance.

- **Equity** – While many equity plans are available, our models provide a formal, structured mechanism to incorporate profit share and equity into any business succession plan. This allows employees to transition into an equity ownership position within their business and encourages long-term strategic thinking.

- **Control** – This step is often never utilised, though, on occasion, it has substantial benefits in terms of succession, not only in terms of ownership but also of business management. This may mean that key employees are able to takeover general management or become CEO of the company. They may also end up with a seat on the board at some future date. However, this step is not to be rushed.

If managed correctly, the ladder is an excellent methodology to identify opportunities to progressively transition employees to think and act like business owners and motivate key employees in the long term. Note, however, that the transition should be managed carefully with KPIs and performance criteria to proceed up the ladder. Such plans can fall over without logical steps for employees or where businesses miss steps trying to fast-track progression.

How can you get your staff to think and act more like business owners?

"Employee ownership is world changing. It is the way ahead... in the global economy. It reflects that human capital is becoming more important than physical assets...The global economy will succeed when employees feel a stake in the business."

Gordon Brown MP
Chancellor of the Exchequer

There are many more exciting and creative options for employee incentive schemes than just paying bonuses. Participation in a business's equity is a crucial component of an effective reward system. While fixed remuneration rewards the individual for performing their duties, and incentive plans help to direct a person's activities, decisions, and behaviours toward the achievement of predetermined short-term goals, a share plan is an essential tool for aligning the employee's personal goals with the business's goals in the longer term.

In July 2015, the Federal Government introduced new measures to encourage and promote ESOPs.

The Government recognised that ESOPs benefit both employers and employees by:

- aligning their interests and goals
- enabling employees to benefit when their employer does well directly and
- enabling employers to benefit from a more committed workforce.

Former Telstra CEO David Thodey said, *"There's no better way to tune people into creating shareholder value than to make them shareholders... I know it gave our people more understanding and a sense of responsibility for what was happening in the company... In my view, it's a win-win."*

In October 2022, introduced a new Divisions 1A into Part 7.12 of the Corporations Act. The new division replaces and expands the ASIC class order relief in relation to employee share schemes.

Specifically, the New Division makes it easier for listed and unlisted companies and listed registered management investment schemes to access 'regulatory relief' from the Corporations Act's securities disclosure (e.g., prospectus), licensing, advertising, anti-hawking and on-sale regulatory requirements in relation to offers of interests under employee share schemes (**ESS interests**).

The New Division cuts previous 'red tape' to provide entities with Australian-based employees and service providers substantially greater flexibility to offer participation in their employee share schemes outside the Corporations Act's existing exemptions from disclosure (e.g., the senior manager exemption and small-scale offerings exemption). This is significant because the previous disclosure exemptions were limited and quickly exhausted, particularly by entities in a high-growth phase that are rapidly expanding their employee base.

Share plans that first provide for the owners to receive an equitable return (profit) on their risk and capital and then allocate a percentage of additional profits to a pool for employees to share in have been found to vastly improve an organisation's profits while promoting teamwork, shared goals, and group achievements. Strategically planned and executed employee share plans can also help businesses, and their staff achieve several other goals, such as succession planning, capital retention, wealth creation, and asset protection.

Succession Planning

There is much recent research on succession planning within SMEs:

1. **KPMG's Australian Family Business Survey 2022** highlights the importance of governance and succession planning. It found that only a minority of family businesses have formal governance structures like family boards or councils. The survey emphasises the need for adaptable leadership styles and focusing on socioemotional wealth to ensure long-term success.

2. **PwC's 10th Family Business Survey** reveals that 30% of first-generation Australian family businesses expect the next generation to become majority shareholders within the next five years. The survey also found that 20% of these businesses prioritise increased involvement of the next generation in decision-making.

3. A new guide released by the **Small Business Ombudsman and Family Business Australia** indicates that only 17% of Australian family businesses have a future plan for their business. This guide aims to help family businesses develop effective succession plans.

4. **The 2023 Family Business Survey by Grant Thornton** shows that 72% of family businesses believe succession planning will be a crucial topic over the next two years.

Over the next decade, the retirement of family business owners will see the transfer of approximately $4.2 trillion in wealth, which surely must make succession planning one of the most significant issues currently facing small business owners.

Employee share can significantly assist in the transition of business ownership. For example:

- In the case of a management buy-out, the ability for staff to acquire equity (through an employee share scheme) can facilitate the transfer of ownership over a period of time, whilst protecting all parties.
- In the case of an external sale, an employee incentive scheme can help increase the business's value; prospective buyers will be prepared to invest more in a business where the employees' financial interests are aligned with the employers.

My book, Enjoy It, covers succession planning in more detail.

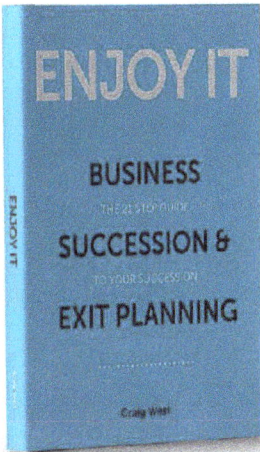

Scan the QR code to download 'Enjoy It'.

Capital Retention

The opportunity to raise capital from within the business rather than from external investors or lenders can be an attractive option. This option enables control of the organisation to remain in-house while allowing employees to share in equity and profits.

Wealth Creation

Contributions to an employee share ownership scheme can offer employees the ability to invest pre-tax dollars, a unique opportunity for wealth creation that is particularly attractive to people with the financial capacity to save regularly, and the tax concessions available can also boost performance.

Asset Protection

Using trusts as investment vehicles can provide asset protection for both employer and employee. Suppose the employer or a participating employee experiences financial difficulties to the extent that funds invested in an employee incentive scheme are held within a trust (rather than by the employer). In that case, those funds will be protected from bankruptcy trustees. (For more about asset protection, request a copy of my book, **Protect It**)

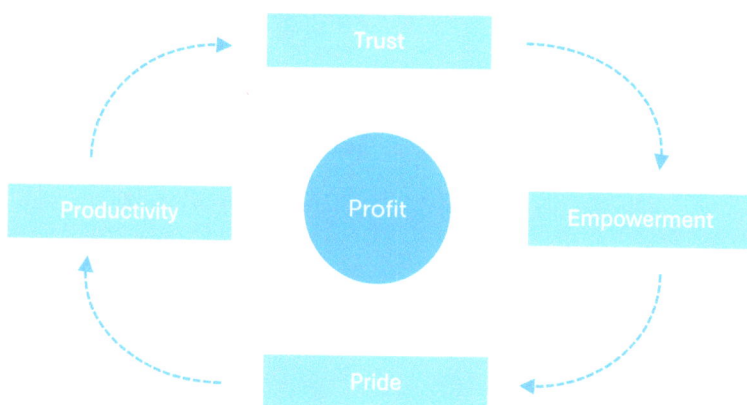

The primary objective of an employee share ownership scheme is to create a structure within which your employees' lifestyle and financial goals are aligned with your business objectives. The result? A cohesive and committed team that is single-minded about working toward and sharing the benefits of a successful and profitable business.

Several employee share and equity vehicles are often used, each with advantages and disadvantages. In the next chapter, we will briefly examine these and then introduce you to a custom-designed type of employee equity plan: the Peak Performance Trust (PPT). It captures the best elements of each option in one unique trust, offered by Succession Plus. The first Peak Performance Trust was implemented in 2006, and it's still running today. This was the first Employee Ownership Trust in Australia, and we now manage more than 130.

Succession Plus ESOP Snapshot

135	1,765
PLANS	**EMPLOYEES**
9.2m+	**$68m+**
SHARES	**EQUITY VALUE**

Common employee equity and share ownership plans

"Only three measurements tell you nearly everything you need to know about your organisation's overall performance: employee engagement, customer satisfaction, and cash flow. No company, small or large, can win over the long run without energized employees who believe in the mission and understand how to achieve it."

Jack Welch, Former CEO of GE

Types of Employee Share Plans

The most common employee equity and share ownership plans are:

- Start-up plans
- Option plans
- Replicator share plans
- Public employee savings plans
- Deferred tax plans.

Let's discuss each of these in general below.

Start-up ESOP Plans

The Turnbull Government introduced these plans as part of the Government Industry Innovation and Competitiveness Agenda. They are simple to set up and use. They also have significant tax advantages for participants, with no upfront tax, no tax at vesting, and no tax on exercise.

Participants are generally only taxed on disposal of shares or options and with a 50% CGT discount.

The Start-up ESOP plans are restricted to businesses that meet all the following conditions for **employers**:
- Not listed on a public exchange
- Aggregated turnover of less than $50m
- Less than ten years old
- Australian resident taxpayer.

Shares must be available to 75% of employees with more than three years of service. In addition, **employees** must also meet the following criteria:
- Must collectively own less than 10% of shares (and voting rights)
- Must be employed by a holding company or subsidiary or subsidiary
- May only receive a 15% or lower discount on shares
- Must hold shares for at least three years.

The plans are not very flexible and do not provide some of the protections we feel are necessary.

Taxation Implications for Start-up ESOPs

The Government introduced changes to the tax treatment of employee share schemes (ESS) on 1 July 2015. These changes apply to ESS interests (shares, stapled securities and rights to acquire them) issued on or after that date.

The main changes announced in 2015 were to:

- the timing of the deferred taxing point for ESS interests acquired under tax-deferred schemes, including increasing the maximum deferral to 15 years
- the test for significant ownership and voting rights limitations have been eased
- that a tax refund is possible in some circumstances where an employee acquires rights but chooses not to exercise them.

Each of these are briefly discussed below.

Deferred taxing point

The taxing point in tax-deferred schemes has become the earlier of:
- when there is no risk of forfeiting the ESS interests and any restrictions on their sale are lifted
- in the case of rights, when the employee has exercised them and there is no risk of forfeiting the resulting share and no restriction on disposing of that share
- when the employee ceases the relevant employment
- 15 years after the ESS interests were acquired (the maximum deferral allowed).

Significant ownership test

The significant ownership and voting rights test have changed. All interests in the company, including rights to acquire shares, are considered (previously only share ownership was considered). However, an employee can acquire up to 10% ownership in the company or control up to 10% of the voting rights before their holding is considered significant, making them ineligible for concessional treatment.

Tax refund

A refund of tax paid at the taxing point is possible if an employee acquires rights and later chooses not to exercise them or allows them to be cancelled. However, as before, a refund is not available if the employee share scheme is structured to directly protect the employee from a fall in the market value of the shares.

Concessions for start-up companies

The discount provided for eligible ESS interests will not be taxed under the ESS regime, if the eligibility criteria are met.

Any gain or loss on disposal of the rights or shares will be assessed under the capital gains tax regime. When working out if the 50% CGT discount applies, the period of ownership of a share acquired on exercise of a right is taken to have started when the right was acquired.

Assistance for start-up companies

There are approved market valuation methods start-up companies can use to value their unlisted shares. These are referred to as a safe harbour valuation and are primarily based on Net Tangible Assets.

We have developed a set of standard documents to help start-up companies establish an ESS, including a performance-based rights plan and a standard letter offering employees an ESS interest in the company.

Options Plans

This plan enables companies to provide equity to principals and key employees. It is best used to reward performance and align employee and company goals. An option contract delivers this and integrates both short – and long-term employee incentives. These plans are often complicated and misunderstood, options are financial derivatives designed for another purpose.

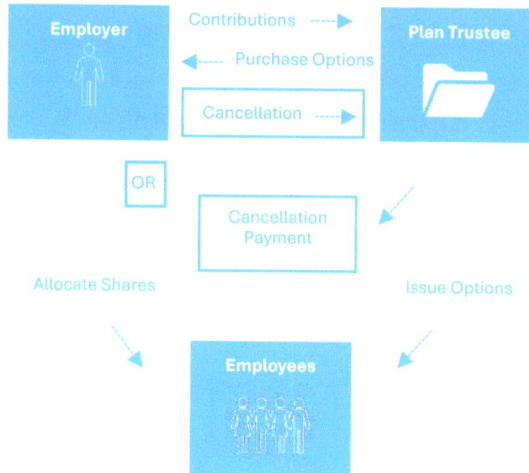

The Options Plan	
Advantages	Disadvantages
• Flexible – facilitates virtually any vesting contingency • Easy to administer • Tax effective, but not tax driven • Efficient and effective delivery of after-tax equity benefits • Administration costs are fully tax deductible to employer • Funding of realised benefits is fully deductible to employer • Employees are eligible for Capital Gains Tax discount on gains • No prospectus obligations	• Options granted to employees are difficult (if not impossible) to value • Options are generally illiquid • Can be difficult for employees that have no experience in trading options to understand

Replicator Plans

This is an employee share plan through which equity can be provided to any or all employees of any size company. This option has the capacity to offer a wide range of investment choices and is designed to provide employees with the benefits of investing in assets that replicate the value of the underlying business.

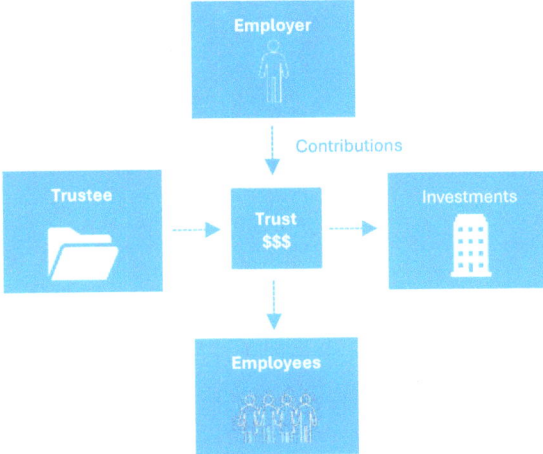

Replicator Plans	
Advantages	**Disadvantages**
• Flexible – facilitates virtually any vesting contingency • Can provide a range of investment options • Offered on a fully administered basis • Easy to understand and communicate • Tax effective, but not tax driven • Efficient and effective delivery of after-tax equity benefits • Administration costs are fully tax deductible to employer • Funding of realised benefits is fully deductible to employer • Employees are eligible for Capital Gains Tax discount on gains • Established wrap-around prospectus precedents	• Difficult (impossible) to accurately replicate the value of the business • Liquidity is uncertain and variable

Public Employee Savings Plan

The most effective savings plan for public-sector and not-for-profit employees is designed to offer employees the opportunity to access the same equity and investment opportunities that are generally available in private-sector employee share plans.

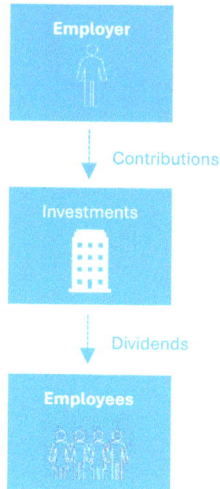

Public Employee Savings Plan	
Advantages	Disadvantages
• Flexible – facilitates most vesting contingencies • Can provide a range of investment options • Offered on a fully administered basis • Tax effective, but not tax driven • Employees are eligible for Capital Gains Tax discount on gains	• Difficult to match equity/income to employee performance • Liquidity is uncertain • Contributions taxed as salary

Deferred Tax Plans – Div 83 A

Deferred taxation means that the employee is taxed on the value of a share or right they acquire under an Employee Share Scheme (ESS interest) at the 'deferred taxing point' (on the market value at that time) rather than at the time they acquire the ESS interest.

Under the current ESS rules, deferred taxation automatically applies to a qualifying ESS interest if either:

- there is a 'real risk of forfeiture' under the scheme or
- there is a 'genuine restriction on disposal' or
- the scheme is a qualifying salary sacrifice arrangement.

Deferred taxation will not apply (and the employee will therefore be taxed up-front) if the employee and their 'associates':

- Holds a beneficial interest in more than 10% of the shares in the company (which includes explicitly shares that the employee can acquire under an ESS interest that is a right to acquire such shares) or
- Can cast or control the casting of more than 10% of the votes that may be cast at a general meeting of the company (which, again, includes the voting power attached to any shares the employee can acquire under an ESS interest that is a right to acquire such shares.

The taxing point only arises when the right is exercised and:

- There is no real risk that, under the conditions of the scheme, the employee will forfeit or lose the share acquired on exercise (other than by disposing of it) and
- There are no genuine restrictions under the scheme for the disposal of the share.

The maximum deferral period under s 83A-120(6) for all ESS interests will be 15 years after acquiring the ESS interest.

The ultimate employee equity ownership plan

"Do you know how much faster I can fix an airplane when I want to fix it than when I don't want to fix it?"

Gordon Bethune

Peak Performance Trust

Introduction

One of the most innovative vehicles to provide employee share ownership is the Peak Performance Trust (PPT) – a type of trust developed by, and only available through, Succession Plus.

The PPT has been developed specifically to meet the needs of small to medium-sized privately owned businesses. If there's any business sector that genuinely benefits from having employees who are motivated to think and act more like business owners, it's SMEs. But until now, employee incentive vehicles like the ones we've just looked at have been designed for large corporates – they're complicated, expensive, difficult to establish and administer, and largely inappropriate for smaller privately owned companies.

After twenty-five years of working with small and medium-sized businesses and understanding their needs, we developed the PPT to offer smaller companies a tool that delivers all the benefits of a sophisticated employee incentive scheme but without the expense or complexity. The PPT is simple, effective and good value for the benefits it brings.

CPA Australia's 'In the Black' magazine described Peak Performance Trusts as an *"ingenious funding mechanism for exit strategies"*.

With a PPT, the employer creates an employee ownership trust into which it makes contributions on behalf of, and for the benefit of, its employees. It commits to investing a predetermined amount of money into the trust regularly, contingent upon participating employees achieving predetermined performance outcomes. The PPT links increased profits to performance payments made into a trust on behalf of employees, building an employee's stake in the business. As the profits increase, so does the percentage share that employees can benefit from. If profits are not increased, no further allocation of funds is made to the PPT.

Participating in a PPT can significantly benefit the employer, the founders and the employees. Unlike any other employee incentive tool, it ties the employee's financial and lifestyle goals to the company's performance. It is the ultimate 'golden handcuff' for your high-performing staff.

From employees to business owners

One of my clients used a PPT to let its employees buy the company from the two founders. The exit plan started early to allow for a gradual sell-down of equity into the PPT for the benefit of most of the employees in the business. The founders gifted 5% of the equity into the plan to start things off. Then, a profit share plan was implemented (replacing all existing bonus schemes), and each time the business achieved profit above a benchmark level, 25 % of those profits were paid into the PPT. The PPT is only able to use those funds to acquire shares, which are purchased from the founders. Every time the team achieved profit of $1 million above the benchmark, the employer would contribute $250,000 into the trust. Staff turnover in this organisation has dropped to an all-time low, and as an unexpected bonus, staff now take extra care and pride in their work, products and customer service. Ten years from now, the asset's value will have increased dramatically, the founders will have sold down all their shares, the business will be 100% employee-owned, and the staff will continue to receive benefits from the trust's income as dividends are paid and distributed.

Using PPTs to fund succession planning

One of the best ways a PPT can benefit the business is to provide a facility to fund an ongoing succession planning arrangement – whereby money set aside within the trust is used to fund the purchase of a proportion of the business. Because the purchase is directly linked to the performance of the business, it becomes largely self-funding. This can also add to the company's value because it can clearly be demonstrated to potential buyers that the employees' future incomes are directly linked to the company's future performance. Many clients use this approach, mainly where most of the business is (and always will be) closely held or family owned. This provides a succession mechanism for key staff who are focused on working with the family to grow the value of the business.

- **Employer Contributions**: Employers can contribute a portion of their profits to the PPT. For example, a company might contribute a percentage of its excess Net Operating Profit After Tax (NOPAT) above a set benchmark.
- **Employee Buy-In**: Employees can purchase units in the PPT using their own funds, drawn down from savings, for example.
- **Salary Sacrifice**: Employees can allocate a portion of their salary to buy units in the PPT (the tax rules currently limit this to $5,000 per person per year).
- **Debt Funding**: External debt funding can finance the purchase of shares in the employer. Banks or private lenders typically provide this funding. They may require security over the shares being funded, a deed of priority for dividends to pay down the loan, and sometimes a personal guarantee from the employee buyer.
- **Profit Share Plans**: Employees can earn equity through profit share plans. The equity earned can serve as a deposit for further acquisition of shares, making it easier for employees to buy additional shares over time.
- **Dividends**: The company can pay dividends to the PPT, which can then be used to acquire more shares (a type of dividend reinvestment plan)
- **Tax-Exempt Shares**: Companies can provide tax-exempt shares to employees as part of their compensation package. These shares can be held within the PPT and contribute to the overall funding (this is also currently limited to $1,000 per person per year under the tax rules).

Each method has its own rules and considerations, and the choice of funding method will depend on the specific goals and circumstances of the employer and employees involved. Of course, it is possible to combine these various methods.

PPT structure

The concept of trusts emerged in medieval England, primarily during the Crusades (11th to 15th centuries). Knights who left for the Crusades needed a reliable way to manage their lands and properties while away. Since women and children could not hold titles, they would transfer their assets to a trusted individual, a trustee, who would manage the property on behalf of the knight and his family. This arrangement separated the legal ownership (held by the trustee) and the beneficial ownership (held by the knight's family).

The trust structure protected assets and ensured the knight's family could benefit from the property even in the knight's absence. This system laid the foundation for modern trusts, which continue to be used for asset protection, estate planning, and managing family wealth. In this example, it is to hold shares for the benefit of employees. The PPT is a particular type of trust where the trust's assets are reflected in units (which are owned by employees) and allows the trust's assets to be apportioned amongst its unitholders.

Using a PPT generally introduces only one new shareholder to the company—the PPT itself. This can significantly simplify the business ownership structure rather than having several individual shareholders, which can lead to minority shareholder issues and cost and compliance problems; the trust becomes the majority shareholder, and the employees become unit holders within the trust. So, the benefits of share ownership can be achieved without complicated ownership structures.

As mentioned previously, PPTs are especially advantageous from a taxation point of view when used solely to fund succession within the business because they become FBT-exempt. See Part 2 for a detailed example of how these benefits apply.

Benefits of PPTs

The benefits of a PPT in succession planning include the following:

- gives the company a competitive advantage in recruiting, motivating and retaining high-performance staff
- affordable for the business
- encourages ongoing profit improvement through rewards linked to performance
- tax effective for both the business and participating employees
- reflects and influences the values and culture of the business
- supports employee development
- rewards employees who make a substantial contribution to the business
- reflects different individual motivations
- is easily understood, controlled and managed
- is appropriate for both the long and short term
- complies with all current and likely Australian taxation and legal requirements
- assists in funding succession planning and new business opportunities
- assists employees in achieving their financial and lifestyle goals.

Features of a PPT

The PPT has the following features:

- An employer or employee makes a request to set up a Peak Performance Trust (PPT).
- The PPT will have a corporate trustee who will manage its affairs (typically, the corporate trustee's directors are the same as those of the business entity).
- Contributions to the PPT can be made by both the employer and one or more employees (see the funding section above).
- Each employee will be invited to join the trust based on predetermined selection criteria and will be allocated units in the trust.

Typically, the employer will agree to contribute to the trust annually based on a profit share formula.

- The trustee (based on the rules outlined in the trust deed) will have strictly limited investment powers, which will restrict the PPT to only investing in shares in the employer entity (or holding company)
- The PPT units will convey the same rights as owning direct shares to the unit holders (i.e. one unit = one share).
- Under the terms of the trust deed, all employee units that are the result of an employer contribution are subject to the disqualifying events and disqualifying discounts (see the technical section in Part 2 for further details)
- The PPT's income (i.e. dividends paid by the employer company to the PPT) must be distributed to unit holders on an annual basis, though this may happen more frequently based on the number of units held by the employee and how often the business pays dividends.

Who can participate in a Peak Performance Trust?

Each PPT is tailored to the needs of each business, and the participation criteria can vary accordingly. However, there will usually be qualifying criteria for participating employees:

- An employee must have worked for the employer for an initial period (for example, twelve months) before being invited to participate as a unit holder in the PPT.
- An employee must continue to work for that employer for a designated period before realising the value of the investment (for example, employees who leave in the first two years may only be able to extract 25 percent of their investment; after three years, 50 percent; and after four years, 75 percent, and so on).
- Notably, one key feature of a PPT, as opposed to some other plans, is that it allows subcontractors to be included in the plan.

How the PPT works

Here is an overview of how PPTs work:

The PPT structure is fairly simple (which is a good thing). The structure provides for indirect or pooled ownership, where the PPT invests in shares in the company, and unitholders (selected employees) become indirect equity holders.

The PPT creates a structure designed specifically for succession planning by transitioning ownership of equity in the company to key employees over a period of time. Using a PPT to fund succession planning offers significant tax advantages, which we explain in detail in Part 2.

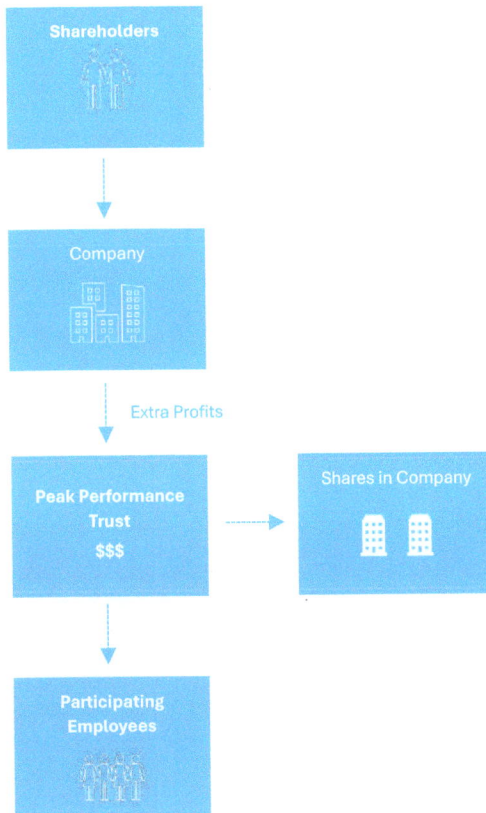

Six easy steps to implementing a PPT in your business

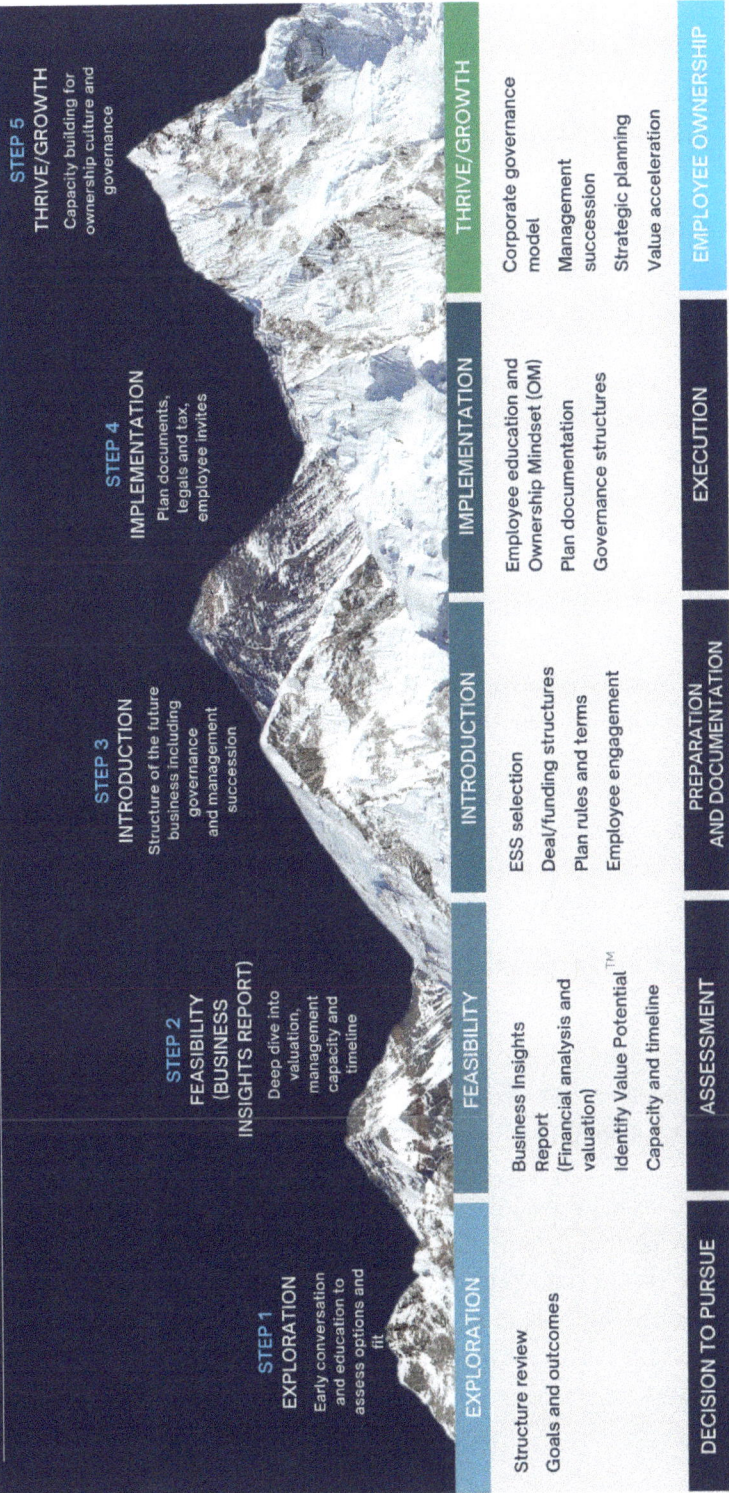

SUCCESSION+   mySharePlan   EMPLOYEE OWNERSHIP

STEP 1
EXPLORATION
Early conversation and education to assess options and fit

STEP 2
FEASIBILITY (BUSINESS INSIGHTS REPORT)
Deep dive into valuation, management capacity and timeline

STEP 3
INTRODUCTION
Structure of the future business including governance and management succession

STEP 4
IMPLEMENTATION
Plan documents, legals and tax, employee invites

STEP 5
THRIVE/GROWTH
Capacity building for ownership culture and governance

EXPLORATION	FEASIBILITY	INTRODUCTION	IMPLEMENTATION	THRIVE/GROWTH
Structure review	Business Insights Report (Financial analysis and valuation)	ESS selection	Employee education and Ownership Mindset (OM)	Corporate governance model
Goals and outcomes	Identify Value Potential™	Deal/funding structures	Plan documentation	Management succession
	Capacity and timeline	Plan rules and terms	Governance structures	Strategic planning
		Employee engagement		Value acceleration

DECISION TO PURSUE	ASSESSMENT	PREPARATION AND DOCUMENTATION	EXECUTION	EMPLOYEE OWNERSHIP

48

Step One: Exploration

The first step in the process is to identify:

- which employees you want to include within the PPT
- which aspects of their performance you plan to focus on, and therefore focus the rules of the trust toward improving.

It is preferable to include as many people in the organisation as possible within predetermined eligibility criteria. The criteria should specify a minimum period of employment, the funding arrangements, and what happens when an employee leaves the organisation. Refer to 'Employee Participation' in Part 2 for more information on employee eligibility considerations.

Because the PPT is such a flexible structure, it can be customised to measure and reward different performance criteria in different businesses. Therefore, it is important to determine which aspects of individual and overall performance you wish to focus on and reward. No more than two or three KPIs are recommended so as not to overcomplicate the process for either yourself or your employees.
While the primary focus of a PPT should always be increasing the value of the business, you can also incorporate a range of other performance metrics, including some that aren't even financial. For example, you could include performance measurements of:

- sales.
- profit.
- customer complaints.
- billable hours.
- punctuality.

The PPT's flexibility enables it to be used to measure and reward both individual and team performance. One of my clients, a mortgage lender, rewards its mortgage broking team leaders first on the profitability of the business overall, second on the number of loans settled by his or her team, and finally on the number of loans he or she individually signs up. This multi-focused approach not only creates incentives for individual performance but also for strong team performance and contributes to the development of highly cohesive teams that are single-mindedly focused on achieving results that allow everyone to benefit.

We then move onto feasibility where we examine the ownership structure and look at which plan is most appropriate.

Step Two: Feasibility & Financial Modelling

Next, it is important to review and model the financial performance of your business to ensure that the KPIs you have chosen are appropriate and will actually drive increased profit. For example, many businesses nominate 'sales volume' as a KPI, but all this does is encourage staff to discount prices to increase sales. The impact on the business is negative.

The best place to begin financial modelling is by looking at your business's current profit drivers. A Business Insights Report (part of the process to implement a PPT) should be able to identify what factors within your remuneration system and fee structure significantly affect the profitability of your business, and these are the areas that the PPT should focus on to motivate improvements. With or without a PPT, all businesses should model their financial performance and identify their key profit drivers to understand what influences their bottom line. If you get this wrong, you'll be focusing on the wrong things; add a PPT to the mix and you'll be providing incentives for your staff to focus on improving the wrong outcomes.

Rigorous financial modelling should also be undertaken to determine the level of profitability within the business and to identify what level of contribution payment can be made to the PPT while still allowing the business's profitability to improve. It is a useless exercise to give away all of the increased profit (the plan must be self-funding).

As part of the PPT implementation program, we prepare a detailed financial model that examines each of these factors and shows the PPT's effect at various performance levels. This allows business owners to determine exactly what their business's financial position will be post-implementation. The following is an example of a strategic forecast model.

At this time, we also need to complete a valuation and examine the value potential of the business. Our main aim is to increase the equity value over time, and we need to make sure this is achievable.

Value Potential

	As of today	Resolve profit gap	Best in Class financials	Attractiveness	Strategic Exit
Revenue	$8,093,000	$8,093,000	$8,093,000	$8,093,000	$8,093,000
EBITDA	$1,576,713	$1,904,701	$1,930,235	$1,930,235	$1,930,235
NOPAT	$1,039,593	$1,255,849	$1,272,685	$1,272,685	$1,272,685
EBITDA Multiple	3.37	3.37	3.37	4.03	4.69
NOPAT Multiple	5.11	5.11	5.11	6.11	7.11
Valuation	**$5.31M**	**$6.41M**	**$6.50M**	**$7.78M**	**$9.05M**

Current Valuation   Potential Valuation

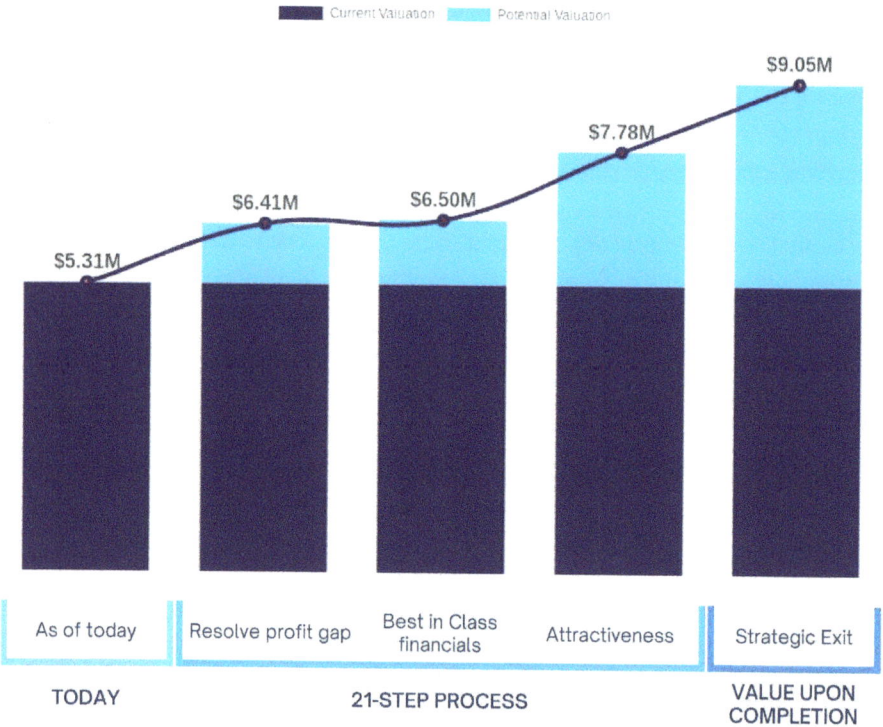

$5.31M $6.41M $6.50M $7.78M $9.05M

| As of today | Resolve profit gap | Best in Class financials | Attractiveness | Strategic Exit |

TODAY   **21-STEP PROCESS**   **VALUE UPON COMPLETION**

The following graph is from the case study used throughout my book "Enjoy It". This book provides you with a step-by-step guide to business succession and exit planning. The business in the case study is Smith Engineering Pty Ltd with Jane and John being the owners. Rod has worked for them for many years. The following graph highlights how the employees (Rod and other managers) benefit after introducing employee incentive schemes, with increased equity in the business for employees. At the same time, there was a decrease in the owners' shares (Jane and John) over five years.

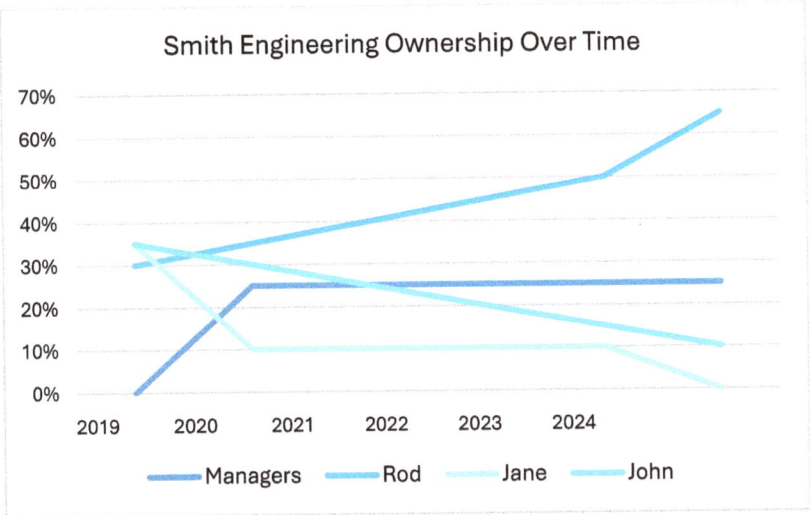

Smith Engineering Ownership Over Time

	2019	2020	2021	2022	2023	2024
Managers	0%	25%	25%	25%	25%	25%
Rod	30%	35%	40%	45%	50%	65%
Jane	35%	10%	10%	10%	10%	0%
John	35%	30%	25%	20%	15%	10%

There is little point in setting up any reward plan if employees don't understand how it works, or if they become discouraged by the plan because of a lack of communication and transparency. A structured internal communications program to launch and report on the PPT on an ongoing basis is essential.

Staff seminars are ideal for introducing the PPT. The objective of these is to educate staff about what the PPT is, how it works, what performance measures it focuses on improving, etc. This usually takes place over two or three separate sessions designed first to help staff understand the concept of the PPT and then the details of the company's specific plan. Staff also receive an employee manual that clearly outlines the operation of the PPT, the legal mechanisms behind it, their rights and obligations as participants, what they can expect on an ongoing basis in reporting and communication, and so on.

For many clients, we also run an Ownership Mindset program, which fosters a culture where employees feel a sense of responsibility and accountability for their work and the organisation's success. The program consists of two 3-hour workshops and covers the following:

1. **Introduction and Objectives**
   - **Purpose**: Explain the importance of an ownership mindset and how it benefits both the employees and the organisation.
   - **Goals**: Set clear objectives for the program, such as improving employee engagement, increasing productivity, and fostering innovation.
2. **Leadership Commitment**
   - **Role Modelling:** Leaders should demonstrate ownership behaviours and set an example for others.
   - **Support:** Ensure that leadership is committed to supporting employees in taking ownership of their work.
3. **Training and Development**
   - **Workshops and Seminars**: Conduct sessions on accountability, decision-making, and problem-solving topics.
   - **Skill Development**: Provide training to enhance skills essential for taking ownership, such as project management and communication.

4. **Empowerment and Autonomy**
   - **Delegation**: Encourage managers to delegate responsibilities and trust employees to make decisions.
   - **Resources**: Provide the necessary resources and support to enable employees to take ownership of their tasks.
5. **Recognition and Rewards**
   - **Acknowledgement**: Recognise and celebrate employees who demonstrate an ownership mindset.
   - **Incentives**: Implement reward systems (ESOP) that incentivise ownership behaviours, such as bonuses or career advancement opportunities.
6. **Feedback and Continuous Improvement**
   - **Regular Feedback**: Establish a system for providing constructive feedback to employees.
   - **Continuous Learning**: Encourage a culture of continuous improvement and learning from mistakes.
7. **Measurement and Evaluation**
   - **Metrics**: Define key performance indicators (KPIs) to measure the program's success.
   - **Evaluation**: Regularly assess the program's effectiveness and make necessary adjustments.

Step Four: Introduction - Introducing the PPT

As part of the implementation, the plan rules must be designed and agreed upon. Multiple levers can be adjusted to create real business outcomes (matching the goals of the business owner). Once the various rules are agreed upon, the documents need to be drafted.

We often discover that clients do not have many of the necessary systems or documents in place in readiness to introduce a PPT. These include up-to-date employment agreements (in many companies, they are old or non-existent) and salary, wage and accounting software appropriate to manage the PPT (often, it's not even adequate for the pre-PPT requirements of the business). We also frequently see gaps within businesses' budgeting and financial modelling – many business owners don't have a handle on their existing financial arrangements and structure or the costings and KPIs that drive their business performance. There is little point in adding new and more complicated systems on top of an already struggling infrastructure, so these issues must be addressed before introducing the PPT.

Step Five: Implementation - Integrating the PPT

Many business owners have experienced the impact of major reforms such as the introduction of the superannuation guarantee charge and the GST, and they understand that changes in the way their businesses operate require staff retraining, new systems, documentation updates, and, in some cases, equipment upgrades. While integrating a PPT is nowhere near as challenging as these significant changes, it will require a new way of doing things to ensure maximum benefit for the business and its employees.

The necessary legal documents are drawn up in preparation for its introduction, and the trust is created. The PPT is a separate legal structure with its own rights and obligations in terms of taxation compliance and regulatory reporting and, therefore, needs to have its own set of accounts, tax returns, and so on. Accounting software programs such as Xero can easily be set up to calculate, manage and report on the PPT. One of the duties of the board of trustees is to ensure that all the compliance issues within the fund are managed and that returns and documents are lodged correctly and on time to ensure that the fund is fully compliant.

For the PPT to achieve its ultimate purpose, not only do the systems, administration and compliance issues need to be managed, but the fund needs to be fully integrated into the business. So, for example, when potential new employees are introduced to the business, they should be told what the PPT is, why it works and how it can potentially benefit them as a vital aspect of the company's employment offering.

One client uses a PPT with a succession plan to actively attract employees into the business. He finds it a distinct advantage in positioning his business as an employer of choice. It is also a valuable lever to incentivise employees rather than relying solely on continual salary increases to reward and retain staff.

Step Six: Value Acceleration

One of the key aims of the plan is to have employees think and act like business owners and help drive the value of the business and this phase is ongoing. Many of our clients see tangible increases on value after the plan is implemented – it is much more likely to occur if twenty people are focused on this rather than just the owners.

Value acceleration can significantly enhance equity value in an Employee Share Ownership Plan (ESOP) company by aligning the interests of employees and the company, fostering a culture of ownership, and driving performance improvements. By implementing value acceleration strategies, companies can maximise their performance and, consequently, the rewards for employees. This alignment not only incentivises employees to contribute to the company's growth and profitability but also ensures that they directly benefit from its success, thereby enhancing employee engagement, retention, and overall company value.

Ongoing communication and management of the PPT is essential. The management of a PPT and its associated payments is very similar to how superannuation is managed, so we advise clients to handle their PPT the same way as their superannuation.

Employees should receive quarterly statements outlining the fund's performance, the contributions they've received, and the investments the trust has undertaken on their behalf. This allows employees to see the tangible benefit of having the PPT, and it becomes more than just some vague concept that they are not aware of or engaged with, as is often the case with other options and share plans.

It is equally important that participating employees have representation on the board of trustees and that all participants are informed about, if not engaged in, major investment decisions.

Following its establishment, ongoing administration is integral to managing your PPT to ensure compliance with taxation law and maximise the benefits to both your business and the trust's unit holders. This process involves us actively helping you and your financial managers and advisers make your PPT work.

Fortunately, our in-house ESOP admin platform, MySharePlan, manages everything for you and your employees.

Your PPT team will also include:

Accountant

Your company accountant will be involved in the process at several stages and must prepare the trust's annual accounts and returns.

Legal Counsel

Preparation of legal documentation is included in the trust's establishment, but some clients also seek advice on these documents from their lawyers.

Investment Adviser

You may decide to engage the services of an appropriately qualified investment adviser to assist employees who are investing in the plan. We can recommend suitable organisations for your consideration.

PART 2

TECHNICAL GUIDE TO PPTs

The inner workings of a PPT

The fundamental principle of the PPT is to reward value accelerating performance, so it is imperative that bonus payments into the trust only occur when profits have increased. Individual performance against predetermined criteria has been achieved.

A PPT should be used as a genuine bonus-earning opportunity for staff, not as a substitute for less-than-competitive base remuneration. Standard pay rates for all personnel should be benchmarked against industry averages annually and assessed against other internal pay rates every two years. With the introduction of a PPT, other discretionary payments to employees should be discontinued, apart from short-term incentive opportunities.

The Trustee

The PPT is managed by a corporate trustee who is responsible for ensuring the trust is managed according to the rules outlined in the trust deed. It is recommended that the directors of the corporate trustee include:

- Employer representative (a director or owner of the company) – often the same directors as the trading entity.
- An independent adviser (accountant, lawyer or representative of Succession Plus).
- As the plan grows, many clients add employee representatives (employees participating in the plan).

Employee Participation

- While the eligibility criteria can be tailored to meet the needs of individual businesses, it is usual to require employees to have served a minimum period of employment before being invited to participate in a PPT, and to remain with the company for a specified period before they can extract the maximum benefit from participation.
- Generally, the minimum service period will be twelve months, however you may wish to alter or waive this condition for certain staff. For example, an employee whose performance has been less than optimal may be placed on a further probationary period. At the same time, you may wish to lessen or waive the twelve-month minimum to attract or retain a particularly high-performing member of staff.

- When employees (with the company's consent) take a period of absence, their PPT account will be frozen, and funds will be made available in accordance with the vesting conditions upon their return.

Issue of Employee Units

Participation in the PPT is by invitation only at the Directors' discretion. Participating employees are allocated units in the PPT based on each person's contributions. The proportion of bonuses allocated to individuals is often determined using a points system, which can be calculated in various ways.

The number of Employee Units issued to an invitee will be determined by the Trustee with reference to the following factors:

- Length of Service (pro rata for permanent part-time) (25%) and excludes any breaks in employment (i.e. leave without pay) but includes all paid leave periods under standard leave entitlements.
- Role/responsibility (50%) – reflected by consideration of current role, with key metrics including current base salary level (FTE) (salary is a proxy variable for role/seniority/responsibility) and
- Performance (25%).

For example, an employee might be allocated one point for every $1,000 in earnings (including incentives) and one additional point for each year of service. This method of points' allocation takes into consideration seniority (based on salary) and loyalty to the company (based on length of service). But there are many other ways that points can be calculated, depending on the needs of the organisation.

In the future, staff may be able to purchase additional Units in the PPT using their own funds.

There are many other ways that units can be allocated, depending on the organisation's needs. For some clients, we have created allocation methodologies based solely on salary. For others, we have created allocations based on multiple considerations; one client uses three measures: overall business profitability, team sales and individual sales. What this does is reward individual, intra-team and inter-team performance. An approach such as this sends a very clear signal to employees about the behaviours and results expected and valued by the organisation, and it drives a very cooperative and well-integrated culture in which everyone works together for mutual benefit.

Additional Investments- Buy-in

In addition to the company-funded contributions to the trust, employees can also make additional individual investments in the PPT. Because the PPT is designed to earn income on its assets, any investments in the trust are considered capital and are, therefore, not taxable in the hands of the trustee.

Investment Loans – Leveraged Buy-in

Employees can borrow to acquire additional equity in the PPT. Any additional contributions made on behalf of employees who borrow (such as bonus payments or salary sacrifice and dividends) can be used to repay the loan. One of the most common uses for investment loans from a PPT is to enable employees to fund succession. Refer to Part 2 for a more detailed explanation of how this works.

Profit share contribution formula – Earn-in

A minimum target (profit benchmark) is determined based on financial modelling for your business.

Once the minimum target is achieved, the company contributes a predetermined amount (for example, 20 per cent) of any additional profits to the ESOP. If the target is not achieved, no ESOP contribution is made. When determining whether the target has been achieved, total turnover and participating profit margin should be calculated so that they reflect actual net collected income and profit – discounts, refunds, and bad debts should be deducted from the calculation of gross revenue.

The board of directors may vary the percentage controls at its discretion if it decides that this is in the best interests of all employees.

Information about the organisation's performance and the PPT should be made available regularly (ideally monthly), together with communication from management explaining where improvements can be made. This information should be displayed prominently throughout the organisation via a screen saver, intranet, internal newsletter, or noticeboard like the model below. Regular and easy-to-understand performance reports enable staff to become engaged in measuring, managing, and improving business performance.

A common misconception among business owners is that they need to provide extensive information, but that's not the case. It is far more effective for staff to understand and be focused on improving the business's key financial drivers. One of my clients, a sales-based business, reports on sales versus targets, which is enough for staff to see where they are going and leads almost directly to improvements in profitability.

Scoreboard - Month of January 2024

Lagging indicators		Target	Forecast	Gap
Susan	NSW sales	$150,000	$225,000	$75,000
Tom	VIC / TAS sales	$180,000	$90,000	-$90,000
Alex	WA sales	$100,000	$95,000	-$5,000
Phil	QLD sales	$50,000	$75,000	$25,000
Calculation	Total Revenue	$200,000	$300,000	$100,000
Alex	Total Cost of Sales	$400,000	$425,000	-$25,000
Calculation	Gross Margin	-$200,000	-$125,000	-$75,000
Owen	Overhead Expenses	$250,000	$225,000	$25,000
Calculation	Profit Before Taxes (PBT)	-$450,000	-$350,000	$100,000
Leading indicators		**Target**	**Forecast**	**Gap**
Maureen	NSW - referral partner meetings	20	35	15
Linda	VIC / TAS - referral partner meetings	40	25	-15
Cyndy	WA - referral partner meetings	40	10	-30
James	QLD - referral partner meetings	40	50	10
Susan	NSW - on-time performance	95%	78%	-17%
Tom	VIC/ TAS - on-time performance	95%	65%	-30%
Alex	WA - on-time performance	95%	90%	-5%
Phil	QLD - on-time performance	95%	98%	3%
Susan	NSW - net promoter score	20	17	-3
Tom	VIC / TAS - net promoter score	20	25	5
Alex	WA - net promoter score	20	20	0
Phil	Qld - net promoter score	20	19	-1

This simple scoreboard clearly shows performance against the business's key indicators – in this case, existing and new client sale percentages, revenue and total cost of sales as well as on-time performance and net promoter scores by state.

Income

Income in the PPT is made up of dividends paid by the company. The PPT and the founders own Ordinary shares, so when the directors declare a dividend, it is paid to the founders and the PPT. This income is distributed to participating employees (the PPT is a pass-through vehicle) when received, based on the number of units held.

Redemption of Units

The Trustee must sell units upon certain events, including when an Employee Unit Holder is no longer eligible to stay in the PPT or when Employee Unit Holders request their Units to be sold.

When this occurs, the employee will be entitled to an Employee Redemption Amount. Employee Redemption Amount means the cash value of the Shares allocated to the remaining Units sold after the application of the Disqualifying Discount, net of any costs related to selling those Allocated Shares.

The employee will be paid the Employee Redemption Amount as soon as practicable following the redemption of the remaining Employee Units. This is estimated to be within six months but will not exceed 12 months. The most recent previous company valuation will be used to calculate the value of the PPT and the employees units.

Good Leaver – Disqualifying discounts

A Disqualifying Discount applies to Employee Units issued within the company PPT to reward longer-term/longevity of service. The Discount is calculated by reference to how long an employee has held an employee unit.

Held Units for	Disqualifying discount
1 Year	90%
2 Years	80%
3 Years	70%
4 Years	60%
5 Years	50%
6 Years	40%
7 Years	30%
8 Years	20%
9 Years	10%
10 Years or more	0%

Each year, the Disqualifying Discount decreases by 10% until year 10, when they can receive 100% of the value of the Units held. For example, if an Employee leaves the PPT in the fourth year after registering their Units, they would be entitled to 40% of the value of their units upon redemption (60 % discount in year 4).

The Disqualifying Discount will not apply:

- Where the Employee Unit Holder's employment with the Applicant is terminated due to retirement or extenuating circumstances as determined and agreed by the company's majority Shareholders.
- To the proportion of Units purchased by the Employee with their own funds, including reinvestment of their share of any dividends.

For example, if an employee had held his Units for 6 years and holds shares worth $10,000, then his redemption amount would be $10,000 x 60% = $6,000.

Bad Leaver - Disqualifying Events

An Employee Unit Holder's Units will be forfeited if they are the subject of a disqualifying event.

Disqualifying Events are outlined in the Trust Deed as unfavourable circumstances where it would be inappropriate to redeem the full value amount of the Units.

A Disqualifying Events clause ultimately protects both company and each employee participating in the PPT by discouraging behaviour that is inconsistent with the PPT's intentions and the efforts of Employee Unit Holders.

Some examples include:

- If, in the reasonable opinion of the Employer, the holder of the Employee Unit commits any fraud, dishonesty, defalcation or gross, willful or serious misconduct in relation to the Employer.
- The holder of the Employee Unit is dismissed from employment by the Employer. For clarity, dismissal does not include retirement, redundancy or genuine resignation.

- It is discovered that the Employee Unit Holder has moved to a competitor while they are still employed by the company. To avoid any doubt, this does not prevent existing employees from moving to a competitor once their units have been redeemed.
- It is discovered that the Employee Unit Holder has been charged with a criminal offence punishable by a gaol term that brings material disrepute or causes the company financial duress.

Valuation

The only asset the PPT is allowed to own is shares in the employer company and so to value the PPT, we need to value the underlying business. Businesses are nearly always valued based on a multiple of earnings, which is the simplest, fairest and easiest way to determine the value of shares or equity in a private company. Publicly listed companies have a price-to-earnings (PE) ratio, and the same methodology applies to small businesses but is referred to as earnings multiple. A calculation of the value of the company shares based on an earnings multiple calculation is undertaken before the commencement of the PPT (using our Business Insights Report), and the same method is used to update the valuation annually.

What are the taxation implications of PPTs?

The taxation treatment which applies to the PPT trust, the employer, and individual employees are detailed in 3 private binding rulings which have been issued by the Australian Taxation Office.

- ATO Ruling 1052166044817 issued 6 September 2023
- ATO Ruling 1052166068699 issued 6 September 2023

A PPT proves to be particularly tax advantageous when it is used for the purpose of funding internal investment into the company, or succession planning.

As mentioned in Part 1, the Government announced further measures in November 2018 to simplify the employee share scheme, increase the value limit of eligible financial products available to employees to $10,000, and introduce the ability for employees to purchase additional products, if they wish.

Taxation Implications for the Employer

According to the Income Tax Assessment Act 1997 (ITAA), the PPT is an Employee Share Scheme as defined by Section 83A and sub-section 995-1(1) of ITAA. Succession Plus designed it for its clients, who are predominantly mid-market professional services businesses, to attract, retain, and motivate key employees.

Deductibility

Contributions paid by the Employer to the Trust pursuant to the Peak Performance Trust Deed will be deductible in accordance with section 8-1 of the Income Tax Assessment Act 1997 (ITAA 1997).

An employer is entitled to a deduction under section 8-1 for a contribution paid to the trustee of a Trust that is either incurred in gaining or producing the Employer's assessable income, or necessarily incurred in carrying on a business for the purpose of gaining or producing the Employer's assessable income ('positive limbs').

However, subsection 8-1(2) prevents such a deduction to the extent that it is a loss or outgoing of capital, or of a capital nature, is a loss or outgoing of a private or a domestic nature, is incurred in gaining or producing exempt income or nonassessable non-exempt income or is prevented from being deductible under a specific provision of the ITAA 1997 or the ITAA 1936 ('negative limbs').

To qualify for a deduction under section 8-1, a loss or outgoing must be incurred.

Although the term 'incurred' is not defined in the legislation, reference can be made to Taxation Ruling TR 97/7 Income tax: section 8-1 – meaning of 'incurred' – timing of deductions (TR 97/7) and Taxation Ruling TR 94/26 Income tax: subsection 51(1) – meaning of incurred – implications of the High Court decision in Coles Myer Finance (TR 94/26).

Broadly, a taxpayer incurs an outgoing at the time the taxpayer owes a present money debt that they cannot escape. Otherwise, a loss or outgoing is incurred when a taxpayer is definitively committed to the loss or outgoing (refer to FC of T v James Flood Pty Ltd (1953) 88 CLR 492).

It is important to establish that the contributions are irretrievable and not refundable, as they will otherwise not be a permanent loss or outgoing incurred.

Timing of Deductions

Contributions paid by the Employer to the PPT according to the Trust Deed will be deductible in the income year in which the Shares acquired from the contribution are allocated to a Participant.

The provision of money to the Trustee of the Trust by the Employer for the purpose of remunerating its employees under the PPT is an outgoing in carrying on the Employer's business and is deductible under section 8-1 of the ITAA 1997.

The deduction under section 8-1 of the ITAA 1997 would generally be allowable in the income year in which the Employer incurred the outgoing but under certain circumstances, the timing of the deduction is specifically determined under section 83A-210 of the ITAA 1997.

Section 83A-210 of the ITAA 1997 provides that if:

(a) at a particular time, you provide another entity with money or other property:

    i.   under an arrangement; and

    ii.   for the purpose of enabling an individual (the ultimate beneficiary) to acquire, directly or indirectly, an ESS interest under an employee share scheme in relation to the ultimate beneficiary's employment (including past or prospective employment); and

(b) that particular time occurs before the time (the acquisition time) the ultimate beneficiary acquires the ESS interest.

then, to determine the income year (if any) in which you can deduct an amount in respect of the provision of the money or other property, you are taken to have provided the money or other property at the acquisition time.

Section 83A-210 of the ITAA 1997 will only apply if there is a relevant connection between the money provided to the Trustee, and the acquisition of ESS interests (directly or indirectly) by the Employer under the relevant PPT in relation to the employee's employment.

An ESS interest in a company is defined in subsection 83A-10(1) of the ITAA 1997 as either a beneficial interest in a share in the company or a beneficial interest in a right to acquire a beneficial interest in a share in the company.

Under the PPT, the beneficial interest in a Share granted to an employee will be an ESS interest. This ESS interest will also be granted under an employee share scheme in relation to the employee's employment.

Consequently, the provision of money to the Trustee to acquire shares in the Employer is for the purpose of enabling the participating employees, to acquire the beneficial interest in Shares. If that money is provided before the Shares are allocated to a Participant, then section 83A-210 of the ITAA 1997 will apply to deny the deduction until the income year in which the beneficial interest in the Share is allocated to the Participant.

Fringe Benefits Tax

Contributions paid by the employer to the PPT does not constitute a 'fringe benefit' as defined in subsection 136(1) of the Fringe Benefits Tax Assessment Act 1986 (FBTAA).

The PPT is an employee share trust, as defined in subsection 995-1(1) of the ITAA 1997, as the activities of the Trust in acquiring and allocating ESS interests meet the requirements of paragraphs 130-85(4)(a) and 130-85(4)(b) of the ITAA 1997 and its other activities are merely incidental to those activities in accordance with paragraph 130-85(4)(c) of the ITAA 1997.

As such, paragraph (ha) of the definition of fringe benefit in subsection 136(1) of the FBTAA excludes the contributions to the Trustee of the Trust from being a fringe benefit.

Therefore, the Employer will not be required to pay fringe benefits tax in respect of the irretrievable cash contributions it makes to the Trustee of the Trust to fund the acquisition of shares.

Anti-avoidance Part IV A

The general anti-avoidance provisions under Part IVA of the Income Tax Assessment Act 1936 (ITAA 1936) do not apply to the scheme described.

The Commissioner will not seek to make a determination that Part IVA of the ITAA 1936 applies to deny, in part or full, any deduction claimed by the Employer for contributions to the Trustee to fund the subscription for or acquisition of shares in the Employer by the Trustee.

For further information, employers should refer to the
ATO Ruling 1052166044817 issued 6 September 2023,
and ATO Ruling 1052166068699 issued 6 September 2023.

This guide provides general information on the payroll tax implications for employers that are incorporated in implementing a PPT, specifically focusing on the $1,000 tax-exempt scheme and the tax-deferral scheme. Payroll tax rules are broadly similar across all states in Australia.

$1,000 Tax-Exempt Scheme

Under the $1,000 tax-exempt scheme, employers are required to pay payroll tax on the value of shares or rights provided to employees, even if it is up to a maximum of $1,000 per employee per year. Whilst this exemption is designed to encourage employee share ownership by reducing the tax burden on employees, this exemption is only for income tax purposes. For payroll tax purposes, the shares or rights provided are still wages for payroll tax purposes.

Tax-Deferral Plans

Generally speaking, the tax-deferral scheme allows employers the choice to elect to defer the time that the shares or rights are included as wages for payroll tax purposes from the 'date of grant' to the 'vesting date'. The payroll tax implications for employers under this scheme are as follows:

1. **Triggering Event:** Payroll tax is generally payable at the time the share 'vests' in the employee. This typically occurs when the employee exercises their rights or sells their shares (as at that time, the employee's interest in the share cannot be rescinded or forfeited).
2. **7-Year Rule:** Employers must include the payroll tax for the tax-deferral scheme at the time of the 'trigger' event or 7years from the date the shares or rights were granted, whichever is earlier. This ensures that the payroll tax is eventually paid, even if the shares or rights are not exercised or sold within the 7-year deferral period.
3. **No Entitlement, No Tax:** If employees are not entitled to receive any 'redemption' payment (e.g. if they leave the company whilst the shares are subject to a disqualifying discount or are a bad leaver), then there will be no payroll tax liability for the employer. Where the employer elects to defer the inclusion of the share or grant was wages for payroll tax purposes to the 'vesting date' and the employee is not entitled to receive their shares (or the redemption payment arising from those shares), the share or grant does not get included as wages in the first place. Where the employer elects to include the share or grant as wages at the date of grant and the employee is no longer entitled to redemption proceeds, the employer can reduce the value of the share or right no

longer entitled from their wages for payroll tax purposes. This provision helps to mitigate the tax burden on employers in cases where employees do not ultimately benefit from the share scheme.

Additional Considerations

Record Keeping: Employers should maintain accurate records of all shares or rights granted to employees, including the dates of grant, exercise, and redemption. This will help ensure compliance with payroll tax obligations and facilitate the calculation of any payroll tax liabilities.

Taxation Implications for the Employee

Does Division 83A apply?

Division 83A of the ITAA 1997 applies to the acquisition of units by the employee from the trustee of the PPT except where the employee acquires additional units for market value consideration.

Division 83A of the ITAA 1997 applies to an employee share scheme (ESS) interest if you acquire the interest under an ESS at a discount.

Section 83A-1 states that your assessable income includes discounts on shares, rights and stapled securities you (or your associate) acquire under an employee share scheme.

Section 83A-10 states that an ESS interest, in a company, is a beneficial interest in a share in the company; or a right to acquire a beneficial interest in a share in the company. An employee share scheme is a scheme under which ESS interests in a company are provided to employees or associates of employees (including past or prospective employees) of the company or subsidiaries of the company in relation to the employees' employment.

The combined effect of section 83A-20 and paragraph 83A-105(1)(a) is that Division 83A (and either Subdivision 83A-B or 83A-C) will apply to an ESS interest if you acquire the interest under an employee share scheme and at a discount.

Where you accept an invitation to acquire units in the trust for no consideration you acquire ESS interests. The combined effect of sections 83A-10 and 130-85 is that your acquisition of the units in the trust is beneficial interests in shares of the company.

Subsection 130-85(4) defines an employee share trust for an employee share scheme as a trust whose sole activities are:

(a) obtaining shares in a company; and
(b) ensuring that ESS interests in the company that are beneficial interests in those share or rights are provided under the employee share scheme to employees, or to associates of employees, of:
   i.   the company.
   ii.   or a subsidiary of the company
(c) other activities that are merely incidental to the activities mentioned in paragraphs (a) and (b).

As the Trust 's sole activities are obtaining shares in the Employer and providing those shares to employees under the PPT, the trust is an employee share trust.

As you have not paid consideration for the units and the value of the units are equal to the value of the underlying shares, you are taken to have acquired the ESS interests at a discount.

The units in the Trust and therefore the ESS interests are provided to you as an incentive by your employer and as such are clearly acquired by you in relation to your employment. Therefore, Division 83A will apply to the acquisition of units by you.

However, where you acquire additional units in the trust and pay market value consideration for such units, neither of the operative Subdivisions of Division 83A will apply to the acquisition of such units. Although the interests acquired meet the definition of ESS interests in section 83A-10 and such interests are arguably acquired in relation to employment, Division 83A will only apply where such interests are acquired at a discount.

Therefore, Division 83A will not apply to any additional units acquired by you at market value.

Timing of taxing point

A taxing point arises under Division 83A of the ITAA 1997 in relation to the acquisition of units by the employee in the income year in which the deferred taxing point arises for the ESS interests acquired by the employee.

Where an ESS interest is acquired under an employee share scheme in relation to the employee's employment and at a discount, section 83A-20 states that Subdivision 83A-B applies to the interest unless Subdivision 83A-C applies.

Subdivision 83A-B applies to include the discount in the year in which an ESS interest is acquired. However, where the conditions in subsection 83A-105(1) are met, Subdivision 83A-C applies and the discount (i.e. the market value of the interest less its cost base) is included in the employee's assessable income in the income year in which the deferred taxing point occurs.

As the scheme is a share scheme and there is no salary sacrifice involved, the conditions which must be met for deferral to apply are those contained in subsections 83A-45(1), (2), (3) and (6) and subsections 83A-105(2) and (3).

You are a current employee of the company and so the condition in subsection 83A-45(1) is met.

Subsection 83A-45(2) applies as only beneficial interests in ordinary shares of the company will be acquired under the PPT.

Subsection 83A-45(3) applies because the company does not have a predominant business of the acquisition, holding or sale of shares.

Additional contributions by the employee

Contributions made by the employee to acquire additional units in the Trust do not constitute the employee's assessable income.

When you acquire additional units at market value you are providing arms-length market value consideration for the acquisition of an asset, namely the unit. The acquisition is neither ordinary nor statutory income and the consideration provided is an outgoing and clearly not assessable.

Disqualifying event

In the event of a disqualifying event occurring in relation to employee units held by the employee section 83A-310 of the ITAA 1997 operates to treat Division 83A to be taken never to have applied to the ESS interests represented by such units.

Section 83A-310 of the ITAA 1997 provides that Division 83A (apart from Subdivision 83A-E) is taken never to have applied to an ESS interest that is a share acquired by an individual under an employee share scheme if disregarding section 83A-310, an amount is included in the individual's assessable income under Division 83A in relation to the share and the individual forfeits the share and the forfeiture is not the result of either a choice made by the individual (other than a choice to cease employment) or a condition of the scheme that has the direct effect of protecting the individual against a fall in the market value of the share.

There are no conditions in the trust deed which could be taken to have the effect of protecting the individual from a fall in the market value of the share.

The only choice that could potentially affect the individual's entitlement to the shares is a choice to cease employment. As such, a choice is excluded from those that would prevent the section from operating. Section 83A-310 will operate to treat Division 83A to be taken never to have applied to the ESS interests represented by such units in the event of a disqualifying event occurring.

CGT upon redemption

The employee will not be liable for capital gains tax on any capital gain made upon the redemption of ordinary employee units unless the redemption of ordinary units occurs after the deferred taxing point for the ESS interest.

Subdivision 130-D of the ITAA 1997 operates to recognise that Division 83A contains the primary rules for taxing gains on ESS interests acquired under employee share schemes and that capital gains and capital losses on such interests should usually be disregarded during the period in which Division 83A applies to them.

In particular, section 130-80 operates to disregard any capital gain or capital loss to the extent it results from a CGT event (other than where the capital gain or loss results from CGT events E4, G1 or K8) if the CGT event happens in relation to an ESS interest you acquire under an employee share scheme and: if Subdivision

83A-C applies to the interest the time of the acquisition is the time when the CGT event happens; or the CGT event occurs on or before the ESS deferred taxing point for the interest.

As Subdivision 83A-C applies to the acquisition of ordinary units, subsection 130-80 disregards the capital gain or capital loss from CGT events that occur from the time of acquisition up until the deferred taxing point.

Once a deferred taxing point arises in respect of a unit, section 83A-125 operates, inter alia, to reset the unit's cost base at its market value unless the deferred taxing point occurs at the time the unit is disposed of.

CGT, upon additional acquisition

Where the employee has paid market value for the acquisition of additional employee units, he will be liable for capital gains tax on any capital gain made upon the redemption of employee units?

As noted above, section 130-80 of the ITAA 1997 only operates to disregard capital gains and capital losses where either Subdivision 83A-B or Subdivision 83A-C applies to the ESS interest.

Where a unit is acquired for market value (i.e. not at a discount), neither Subdivision 83A-B or 83A-C will apply. Consequently, the acquisition of the units (and underlying shares) will constitute an acquisition of a CGT asset to which section 109-5 of the ITAA 1997 and the remainder of Part 3-1 and Part 3-3 will apply.

Anti-avoidance Part IVA

The general anti-avoidance provisions under Part IVA of the ITAA 1936 do not apply to the scheme described.

A consideration of all the factors referred to in subsection 177D (2) of the ITAA 1936 leads to the conclusion that the dominant purpose of the scheme is to provide remuneration to you in a form that promotes the Employer's business objectives rather than to obtain a tax benefit.

Accordingly, the Commissioner will not make a determination that Part IVA of the ITAA 1936 applies to deny, in part or full, any tax benefit derived by you as a result of your participation in the PPT as described.

Employees can refer to
ATO Ruling 1052166044817 issued 6 September 2023,
and ATO Ruling 1052166068699 issued 6 September 2023
for further information.

Taxation Implications for the Trustee

Contributions to the Trust - employee

Amounts contributed to the trustee by employees for the acquisition of additional employee units do not constitute assessable income of the PPT. These amounts are capital and not assessable income.

Contributions of monies by employees subscribing for additional units in the trust to the trustee pursuant to the trust deed represent the trust's corpus. The contributions constitute capital receipts to the trustee and are not included in the calculation of the net income of the trust estate under section 95 of the ITAA 1936.

Contributions to the Trust - employer

Amounts contributed by the employer to the PPT for the benefit of employees do not constitute income of the Trust. These amounts are capital and not assessable income.

According to the trust deed, the employer's contributions to the trustee represent the trust's corpus. The contributions constitute capital receipts to the trustee and are not included in the calculation of the trust estate's net income under section 95 of the ITAA 1936.

Anti-avoidance – Part IVA

The general anti-avoidance provisions under Part IVA of ITAA 1936 do not apply to the scheme described. Provided that the scheme is implemented as described in this ruling, the Commissioner will not seek to make a determination that Part IVA of the ITAA 1936 applies to deny, in part or full, any tax benefit derived by the trustee because of his participation in the PPT as described.

A consideration of all the factors referred to in subsection 177D (2) of the ITAA 1936 leads to the conclusion that the dominant purpose of the scheme is to provide remuneration to participants in a form that promotes the Employer's business objectives rather than to obtain a tax benefit.

Accordingly, the Commissioner will not make a determination that Part IVA of the ITAA 1936 applies to deny, in part or full, any tax benefit derived by any of the participants, including the trustee, because of their participation in the PPT as described.

The PPT trustees should refer to
ATO Ruling 1052166044817 issued 6 September 2023,
and ATO Ruling 1052166068699 issued 6 September 2023
for further information.

Where to from here?

"If you treat staff as your equals, they will roll their sleeves up to get the job done."

John Ilhan

Once you have decided to implement a PPT within your company, the process is relatively fast; you could have your PPT up and running within as little as a month. A typical implementation timetable would include the following steps:

1. Agree on proposal
2. Agreement recorded and invoice paid
3. Scoping meeting
4. Design
   4.1 Finalise critical PPT criteria:
      4.1.1   Vesting conditions
      4.1.2   Qualifying conditions
      4.1.3   Profit benchmarks
      4.1.4   Trustee board membership
5. Documentation
   5.1 Instruct documentation
      5.1.1   PPT checklist and order form
      5.1.2   Review terms and criteria
   5.2 Documents issued
      5.1.3   Trust deed
      5.1.4   Operating manual
      5.1.5   Administration forms and templates
      5.1.6   Employee handbook
6. Education
   6.1 Staff seminar
      6.1.1   Overview to all staff
      6.1.2   Distribute and review employee handbooks
      6.1.3   Q & A session
7. Activation
   7.1 Finalise execution and implementation
8. Ongoing maintenance
   8.1 ESOP Administration
   8.2 Taxation Lodgments
   8.3 Annual Valuation Update
   8.4 Employee Access to MySharePlan
   8.5 Advice/Queries as required throughout the year
   8.6 Access to Monthly Webinar Series
   8.7 Tickets to Succession Plus's Annual ESOP Conference

FAQs on Employee Share Ownership Plans

1. **Will implementing a share plan mean I need to hand over control of my business?**

   A: NO. ESOPs are not designed to transfer control (until you are ready). They are intended to transition equity to your employees to better align your interests with theirs. In most cases, we use a corporate trustee for the ESOP, and the directors of the corporate trustee (which manages the ESOP) are the same as the main trading entity.

2. **Do my employees expect to pay to join?**

   A: In most cases, we can design the plan so the employees can contribute, but we usually recommend that this is not compulsory—otherwise, you might preclude good employees who simply cannot afford to write out a cheque to participate.

3. **How does this affect the normal laws regarding employment/ HR?**

   A: The introduction of an ESOP does not change the employment relationship, and all the normal HR laws apply to employees who are members of an ESOP.

4. **How much equity do I need to sell down?**

   A: The taxation law governing ESOPs does not have hard and fast rules (and no limits imposed). We have implemented plans with as little as 10% of shares held by the ESOP and some where the ESOP is gradually buying the whole business (100 %).

   The amount you sell needs to be substantial enough to be valuable to employees and provide a reasonable stake in the business.

5. **How do buyers view a business with an ESOP?**

A: In most cases, this is a strong advantage. In many businesses, the critical risk from a buyer's point of view is the risk of employees leaving immediately after a sale. While the ESOP cannot stop this, it can reduce the risk by locking employees in with an equity stake. Many plans introduced in the lead-up to the sale include a stay bonus – an extra contribution made to the ESOP if, for example, employees stay for 24 months after the sale. Sometimes, the buyer will already have an ESOP and roll your employees into their plan. Many will continue the existing plan, while in some cases, the buyer may choose to pay out the plan.

FAQs on ESOPs by Employees

1. **What is my risk? What if the company owes money?**

A: Employees who are members of an employee share plan are protected from any of the liabilities of the employer company and would not be liable for any debts or monies owed. Nor are they required to contribute to any losses incurred by the company.

2. **Can I own the shares in a family trust or my self-managed super fund?**

A: In the Peak Performance Trust, employees can nominate the units to be held by an associate (usually a family trust or company). In most cases, the answer is NO. Unfortunately, many of the benefits are only available to employees, so the shares or options must also be owned by the employee in their own name, in some other structures.

3. **Does being a member of an employee share plan affect the terms of my employment?**

A: NO. The share plan rules, and qualifying conditions relate only to the employee share plan and do not affect the laws that govern your employment, including any enterprise bargaining agreement, award or other arrangement.

4. **If the share plan earns dividends from my employer, do these come to me and if so, do I pay tax on them?**

A: YES. In all the various structures, the employee share plan would typically act as a "flow through" vehicle, and in the case of the trust structure that is commonly used, any income or distributions received need to be passed through to the individual employees and paid in cash. At that point, they would be taxed as part of the employee's income at marginal tax rates. In many cases, dividends include franking credits, which also "flow through" to the employee and reduce the tax payable on the dividend income.

5. **What happens if I leave the company?**

A: Except in very specific and unusual circumstances, leaving employment would trigger redemption. In most plans, this means that you can no longer receive shares or options as you are no longer an employee. In many cases a disqualifying discount also accompanies a disqualifying event, and so the value of your shares or options may be reduced, especially if you "leave early."

6. **Am I now a company director or entitled to a seat on the board?**

A: NO. The employee share plan does not include the right to become a company director. Most employees want to avoid becoming directors, which may make them liable in other areas. Typically, when a share plan becomes a majority owner in the company, then the share plan may have the right to elect an employee to join the board of directors. This, though, is a matter of agreement between the employees and the current directors/founders of the company.

7. **What information will I receive on the performance of the company?**

A: Employee share clan members will always receive an annual statement showing the number of units they hold and the underlying value of the company's shares. The plan administrators will need to complete an annual valuation of the business as part of this process, which will always include a review of financial statements. Most employers provide a summarised version of this information to ESOP members.

8. **What happens if the company is sold?**

    A: If the company is sold externally, there are three possibilities:
    - (a) Members of the employee share plan are "forced" to sell at the same time as the founders (drag along) and would, therefore, be paid out the value of their shares at the time of the sale.
    - (b) The buyer decides to keep the employee share plan in place and continues to make contributions, etc., in the same way the original owners did.
    - (c) The buyer elects to "rollover" employees into their own employee ownership plan

ESOP Myths

1. **Myth: ESOPs are only for large companies** – Many believe that ESOPs are only suitable for large corporations, but they can also be highly beneficial for small-to-medium enterprises (SMEs). ESOPs can help with succession planning, asset protection, and sharing wealth among key employees.

2. **Myth: ESOPs are too complex to implement** – While setting up an ESOP does require careful planning and legal considerations, with the right guidance and expertise, it can be a straightforward process. Many businesses have successfully implemented ESOPs with the help of specialists.

3. **Myth: ESOPs are expensive** – The cost of setting up an ESOP can vary, but the long-term benefits often outweigh the initial expenses. ESOPs can lead to increased employee engagement, productivity, and loyalty, which can positively impact the company's bottom line. The PPT costs approx. 50% of the cost of one employee leaving.

4. **Myth: ESOPs dilute ownership too much** – While ESOPs do involve sharing ownership with employees, the dilution of ownership can be managed effectively. Business owners can structure the ESOP to retain control while still providing significant benefits to employees.

5. **Myth: ESOPs are only for retiring owners** – ESOPs are often associated with succession planning for retiring owners, but they can also be used as a tool for employee retention, motivation, and business growth at any stage of the company's lifecycle.

6. **Myth: ESOPs don't provide enough financial benefits to employees** – ESOPs can be a powerful tool for wealth creation for employees. By owning a stake in the company, employees can benefit from the company's growth and profitability, leading to increased financial security.

7. **Myth: ESOPs are not flexible** – ESOPs can be tailored to meet the specific needs and goals of the business and its employees. There are various ways to structure an ESOP to align with the company's objectives and employee expectations.

8. **Myth: ESOPs are not well understood by employees** – With proper communication and education, employees can fully understand and appreciate the benefits of an ESOP. It's important for companies to provide ongoing support and information to ensure employees are engaged and informed.

PART 3

PPTs IN ACTION: CLIENT CASE STUDIES

These PPT examples are based on real client case studies. While the details of their arrangements are accurate, some names have been changed or omitted to protect client privacy.

Case Study: Construction Project Management Peak Performance Trust

Overview

The Construction Project Management Peak Performance Trust (PPT) was developed to initially replace a poor short-term incentive bonus scheme and improve retention. It succeeded beyond initial expectations due to the alignment of the participants with the company success. From here the Board elected to accelerate participation by allowing employees to directly purchase units. The expected result is gaining overall better shareholder value. The exit and transitioning of founding shareholders are just a bonus. The primary objective of the PPT is to attract, retain, and motivate key employees, creating a succession model that safeguards business stability while maximising value to all.

Key Components

- **Business Succession & Exit Planning:** The PPT operates as part of a broader business succession and exit strategy, built around a 21-step plan designed to evaluate, protect, and maximise business value. This plan integrates understanding of both the financial health of the business and the motivations of the owner(s). The PPT ensures that succession planning is well-structured and that key employees are incentivised to stay through this transition, contributing to the long-term success of the business.
- **Employee Participation:** Employees have the opportunity to acquire units in the trust, which function similarly to shares in the business. These units are part of a profit-sharing mechanism, whereby employees receive annual contributions and dividend distributions tied to the financial performance of the company. This ownership model not only helps in retaining talent but also aligns employee performance with business success, providing employees with a tangible stake in the company's growth.
- **Implementation and Structure:** The PPT is structured as a unit trust, with critical roles and responsibilities clearly defined. The trust operates with a transparent mechanism for employees to acquire units, participate in profit-sharing, and benefit from dividend distributions. By offering ownership stakes, the company creates a compelling reason for employees to remain invested in the business's long-term success.

- **Strategic Overview:** The alignment of employee interests with the company's objectives ensures that employees are both motivated to stay and committed to improving their own financial futures through their investment in the company. This strategic alignment strengthens the overall stability of the business, as employees are more engaged and invested in driving growth and maintaining performance standards.
- **Financial Impact of the PPT:** The introduction of the PPT has demonstrated success in terms of both employee participation and the company's financial growth. Below are key financial metrics in the last three years, highlighting the increase in value and the role the PPT has played in this growth so far:

FY	Number of employees in PPT	Dividends Paid to PPT	Unit price	No. of units in PPT	Total PPT value	Total Issued shares in company	Total company value	PPT %
2023	-	-	$4.28	-	-	3,000,000	$12,842,940	0.00%
2024	46	$34,532	$5.10	76,345	$389,359	3,000,000	$15,300,000	2.54%
2025	68		$8.92	112,861	$1,006,720	3,000,000	$26,747,925	3.76%
						Value increase	108%	

Results

In FY2023, the PPT was not yet active, with no units issued and no participation from employees.

By FY2024, 46 employees had joined the PPT, receiving $34,532 in dividends, with the unit price increasing to $5.10. The total value of the PPT was $389,359, representing 2.54% of the company's total value.

In FY2025, the company offered an additional 112,861 units to 68 employees, bringing the PPT's total value to over $1 million, with a unit price of $8.92. The company's value increased to $26.74 million, reflecting an impressive 108% growth in value over two years, partly driven by employee engagement and ownership.

Conclusion

The Construction Project Management Peak Performance Trust has proven to be an effective tool in driving business succession, retaining key talent, and fostering business growth. By providing employees with equity stakes, the trust aligns their personal financial interests with the company's success. As a result, the PPT has helped improve business performance, increase company value, and ensure a smoother, more secure transition as part of the broader exit planning strategy.

Managing Director and major shareholder James Long recently reflected on the impact of the PPT:

"The PPT is a deceptively elegant system. There is a lot of psychology at play if you set it up well and spend time with education of the workforce.

My experience was that I was initially sceptical as I was brought up on the adage that 'good employees get good wages not equity'. This served me well for 20 years but to accelerate growth I needed a new paradigm.

Previously I had a system of absolutely discretionary bonuses which was OK for a 30-employee organisation. When we reached 60 people, the then executive proposed, and the board approved, the standard short-term incentive program (STIP) or 'bonus' linked to performance against the agreed budget. This created behaviours that were against our normal culture and created misalignment between shareholders and employees, especially when it came to setting the next year's budget. This is a common problem expertly explained in Chapter 12 of Jack Welch's book 'Winning'.

I initially only accepted the premise of PPT as a replacement incentive and retention program to solve the problem above. We converted all our STIP and cash bonuses into a "gifting" of units in the PPT. I analysed the PPT framework and was looking at KPIs to set targets. In the end I felt any financial KPIs are poor when compared to the 'KPI' of the dividend and share price which through the PPT was aligned between the employees and the shareholders. The retention component is due to the pretax nature of the investment and the employee entitlement table. It was a huge success and quickly aligned all parts of the business.

I am now comfortable that the units in the PPT will be a good investment for the employees and as such I am expanding the participation in the PPT so that employees can directly purchase units with their own money.

I am a very analytical person and tore the Succession Plus model apart over 6 months. After all this I have come back to the original model proposed and realised that there are a lot of clever motives baked into the simplicity of the model. My advice is the simpler the model is, the better it is.

Also, you can use it as an incentive and retention model by itself but once you do this it is likely you will extend it to direct employee purchase as the shareholder value will increase quicker."

Case Study: Barker Ryan Stewart's Peak Performance Trust

Overview

The Barker Ryan Stewart Peak Performance Trust (PPT) is an Employee Share Ownership Plan (ESOP) designed to allow employees to own a part of the company they work for. This initiative aims to foster a sense of ownership among employees, encouraging them to think and act like business owners. The trust, known as 'Barker Ryan Stewart Nominees Pty Ltd ATF Barker Ryan Stewart Peak Performance Trust,' invites qualifying employees to participate by owning Employee Units in the PPT.

FY	Number of employees in PPT	Dividends paid to PPT	Unit price	No. of shares held by PPT	Value of PPT shares	Total issued shares	Company valuation	PPT %
2020	9	$1,272	$49.86	7,407	$369,313	120,000	$5,983,499	6.17%
2021	21	$122,263	$65.26	8,329	$543,550	120,000	$7,831,773	6.94%
2022	21	$39,629	$64.42	12,671	$816,265	120,000	$6,825,460	10.56%
2023	26	$129,683	$107.18	15,036	$1,611,558	120,000	$12,861,582	12.53%
					Value increase	115%		

Dividend Distribution

Any dividends received by the PPT are distributed to Employee Unit Holders as cash payments. This ensures that employees benefit directly from the company's financial success, and benefit form franking credits on the dividends.

Performance Tracking

The PPT tracks key metrics such as output per employee and task completion rates to evaluate the impact of the ESOP on productivity. This data is used to develop and track the effectiveness of improvement strategies.

Long-Term Wealth Accumulation

Employees are encouraged to make regular contributions to the ESOP, with resources and support provided to educate them on the benefits of long-term investing. The growth of ESOP accounts is tracked and benchmarked against industry standards.

The PPT has been designed to enhance employee engagement and motivation by recognising and rewarding top performers. Regular satisfaction surveys are conducted to gather feedback and develop strategies for improvement. This approach ensures that employees remain engaged and motivated, contributing to the overall success of the company.

CEO Andrea McDonald said recently that *'the PPT has been a great mechanism for rewarding key staff and allowing employees to purchase equity in the BRS business. The PPT has assisted with the continual development of a cohesive and committed team, sharing the benefit of a successful and profitable business.'*

Conclusion

The Barker Ryan Stewart Peak Performance Trust (PPT) is a strategic initiative that aligns the interests of employees with those of the company. By providing employees with a stake in the company's success, the PPT fosters a culture of ownership and accountability, leading to improved productivity and long-term wealth accumulation for employees.

Background

In 2017, Umwelt implemented an Employee Share Ownership Plan (ESOP) to recognise and reward their employees for their commitment and valuable contribution to the business. Initially, the plan involved 40 members who collectively owned 14% of the company's equity. There was an initial gifting of 10% into the ESOP, recognising that more than 50% of the ESOP entrants had over 10 years of service at Umwelt, at that time. Over the past seven years, the ESOP has expanded significantly, with 126 members owning 47% of the company. The founders had agreed that the most appropriate succession plan was for the employees to own the majority of the business over time.

Growth and Success

Umwelt's experience with its ESOP has been characterised by remarkable growth and success. Starting from a modest 14% employee ownership, the plan has expanded to greater than 47%, reflecting the substantial contribution from the team (many of the Associates have purchased equity over and above the contributions funded by the profit share plan). The business has also grown substantially over that time and now employs more than 300 staff.

Financial Impact

During this period, Umwelt's valuation grew significantly by over 700%, demonstrating the financial success of engaging employees with an ownership mindset, to collaborate on, and deliver, the business strategy. The ESOP has provided financial benefits to the company and enhanced employee engagement and morale.

Employee Engagement

The ESOP has been an important part of fostering a dedicated and invested workforce at Umwelt. The sense of ownership among employees has contributed to overall business success. The plan has been well-received by the Umwelt team, with substantial support and participation. Employees regularly make suggestions for improvement and are actively engaged in the business.

Managing Director, Barbara Crossley, said recently that *'it's fantastic to see employment ownership and participation in the ESOP increase as we continue to grow and evolve the business. As we work through opportunities and challenges, we see our team work together with a 'best for business' approach, and strong commitment to delivering for our clients and achieving our business goals. I am so very pleased to see our employees have the opportunity to share in our success, through the ESOP.'*

Umwelt's transition to employee ownership highlights the profound impact of shared commitment on a company's success. As one of the company's employee-owners expressed, *"I think fundamentally for me, it makes me feel like I'm effectively an owner of the organisation and the actions I undertake day-to-day have broader ramifications for the company's success."*

Conclusion

For businesses considering an ESOP, Umwelt's story illustrates the potential for fostering a dedicated, invested workforce that contributes to overall business success. The significant growth in employee ownership and the company's valuation highlights the financial and engagement benefits of implementing an ESOP.

Introduction

The **Viridian Financial Group Ltd Employee Share Ownership Plan (VFGL ESOP)** is the preferred remuneration and incentive planning model used to reward, retain, and motivate employees who contribute to the business's success. The ESOP provides employees with the opportunity to own equity in the company they work for, aligning their interests with the company's long-term goals.

Objectives of the ESOP

The ESOP was developed with three key objectives in mind:

- **Attracting and Retaining Talent:** By offering equity ownership, Viridian aims to attract and retain key employees, ensuring the company's continued growth and success.
- **Motivating Employees:** The ESOP serves as a mechanism to motivate employees by giving them a stake in the company's success, fostering a sense of ownership and commitment.
- **Succession Planning:** The ESOP is part of a broader business succession plan, ensuring a smooth transition of ownership and management over time.

Key Features of the Plan

The Viridian ESOP includes several key features:

- **Profit Share Model:** Employees can acquire shares through a profit share model, aligning their interests with the company's profitability.
- **Employee Buy-in:** Employees have the option to buy shares, further increasing their ownership stake in the company.
- **Annual Review:** The ESOP is reviewed annually to ensure its effectiveness and alignment with the company's goals.
- **Governance and Administration:** The ESOP is governed by the company's Board of Directors and includes provisions for costs, taxation, and support.

Implementation and Performance

The implementation of the Viridian ESOP has been successful, with over 160 Viridian employees actively participating in company ownership in multiple ways, including electively purchasing and salary sacrificing their wages to purchase equity. The Viridian Employee Share Ownership Plan is now in the top 10 shareholders of the company. The ESOP has contributed to the company's growth and value, with multiple employees achieving significant growth post-implementation.

One of the key challenges faced by the ESOP was accelerating employee buy-in through debt funding. Traditional banks found this difficult, but Viridian developed a vehicle to provide this funding, enabling employees to purchase equity more quickly.

Conclusion

The Viridian Employee Share Ownership Plan has proven to be an effective tool for attracting, retaining, and motivating employees while also serving as a critical component of the company's succession planning. The ESOP's success is evident in the significant employee participation and the substantial value of shares owned by employees.

CEO Glenn Calder said recently, *"We are believers that to align your company vision requires people to connect and identify with it. Ownership is one of the best ways to 'walk the talk' and an effective ESOP is the best way of achieving the goal. Make it visible and accessible and it will help inspire future leaders in more ways than you know."*

Introduction

The company's Employee Share Ownership Plan (ESOP) is designed to reward, retain, and motivate employees by providing them with an opportunity to acquire equity in the company. This plan is implemented through the Peak Performance Trust (PPT), which serves as the mechanism for distributing shares to eligible employees.

Objectives

The primary objectives of the ESOP are:

- To enhance employee engagement and loyalty by offering a stake in the company's success.
- To align the interests of employees with those of the company and its shareholders.
- To provide a competitive remuneration and incentive model that attracts and retains top talent.

Key Features

1. **Equity Allocation:** The PPT can acquire up to 20% of the issued shares of the company. This percentage is subject to regular review and can be increased by the directors if deemed necessary.
2. **Dividends:** Shareholders within the PPT are entitled to dividends paid by the company. These dividends are distributed to eligible employee unit holders based on the number of units they own. For example, if the company declares a dividend of $1,000,000, the PPT will receive a proportionate share, which is then distributed to the employees.
3. **Redemption of Units:** Employees can redeem their units under certain conditions, such as disqualifying events or upon leaving the company. The redemption process and conditions are outlined in the trust deed.
4. **Governance and Administration:** The PPT is governed by a trust deed, which provides the ongoing governance framework. The administration of the PPT includes managing costs, taxation, and providing support to participating employees.

The ESOP is implemented through a structured process that includes:

1. Annual Contributions: Ongoing contributions to the ESOP to acquire shares.
2. Performance Metrics: Regular evaluation of the plan's performance and its impact on employee engagement and company success.
3. Annual Review: A comprehensive review of the ESOP to ensure it meets its objectives and aligns with the company's strategic goals.

When the plan was first set up in 2019, it included just five employees, who acquired 0.86% of the equity in the business through the profit share mechanism. In 2024, the PPT includes 25 employees, including 2 who have purchased equity in addition to the profit share plan. The plan now owns 3.11 % of the business which is equivalent to $3.5 million in equity held by employees.

Conclusion
The company's Employee Share Ownership Plan is a strategic initiative aimed at fostering a culture of ownership and engagement among employees. By providing a stake in the company's success, the ESOP aligns the interests of employees with those of the company, ultimately driving performance and growth.

Case Study: WA Law Firm - Peak Performance Trust

Investment Strategy

The PPT for the law firm employs a straightforward strategy: it exclusively purchases direct shares in the business. This approach grants participating employees an indirect ownership of the business's equity.

Employee Benefits

Participating employees benefit from two key incentives:

- **Dividends:** Employees receive dividends based on the profit performance of the legal practice.
- **Capital Gains:** In the event of a sale of the business, the PPT would share in the capital sale proceeds, indirectly passing a portion of the capital gains to the employees.

Value Linkage

The value of the PPT is directly linked to changes in the value of the business. As the business's value increases or decreases, largely driven by profit performance, the value of the PPT adjusts accordingly. This means employees are directly impacted by and can influence the company's value through their performance.

Conclusion

This simple and transparent PPT strategy ensures that the employees have a vested interest in the business's success, creating a strong link between their efforts and the overall performance of the practice.

Case Study: NSW Accounting Firm - Peak Performance Trust

Background

Like many professional practices, this firm faced challenges in funding key staff into partnership roles. The staff members identified as having the most potential for partnership were often in their thirties – a stage of life where financial resources are often stretched due to personal commitments such as marriage, children, and home purchases. These life circumstances made it difficult for them to afford the purchase of equity in the practice.

The Solution: PPT for Succession Funding

To address this challenge, the practice introduced a Peak Performance Trust (PPT) specifically designed to provide succession funding. This allowed selected staff members to accept partnership opportunities without the immediate financial burden, giving them the chance to invest in the practice over time.

Future Partnership Opportunities

The PPT also served as a motivational tool for "rising stars" within the firm, showing them that partnership was not only a possibility but something they could realistically aspire to. This has created a clear career path for talented staff members and helped foster long-term commitment.

Impact on Business Value and Talent Attraction

By offering succession funding through the PPT, the practice has not only increased its overall value but has also gained a distinct advantage in attracting new senior staff. The ability to offer partnership opportunities with built-in funding has made the practice an attractive destination for top talent in the industry.

Austbrokers Countrywide CEO, Tim Considine, said of the employee ownership model recently, *"the PPT is such a valuable way to release equity within the business at the same time complimenting any larger transactions that occurs within the business."*

LJ Hooker Commercial real estate office on the Central Coast was the Winner of the 2011 ESOP of the Year award using a Peak Performance Trust. The award was based on a substantial reduction in sick days, improved staff retention, and a noted increase in performance and participation.

Ty Blanch of LJ Hooker said, *"We have created a more understanding team of people and added value to the individual's performance congruently.*

Both financial services and property management referrals from employees participating in this scheme increased at a higher level than before. I put this down to their seeing value in contributing to the company's bottom line because they will share in the profit."

The National Personnel Group said, *"Since kicking off our Ownership Thinking program, absenteeism has already dropped by at least one-third! Overall, productivity is higher, and our employees are taking more interest in the financial well-being of the business."*

In discussing the transformative effects of implementing an Employee Share Ownership Plan at an IT company in Perth, the employees shared their insights on the positive cultural shift it has fostered within the company: *"It's just created a really good vibe in the office and it's so positive. People who are able to be part of our ESOP are suddenly thinking about themselves very differently. They're talking about passive incomes, something they've never thought of before in the sense that I can own something, I can actually own where I work."*

GLOSSARY

Allocate Shares

The process of distributing shares to individuals or entities.

Balance sheet

A detailed statement summarises a business's assets and liabilities and gives a picture of its wealth at a particular time.

Base Remuneration

The basic salary or wage paid to an employee.

Capital

The accounting concept of capital refers to the company's issued capital and retained earnings, representing the owners' or shareholders' initial contribution to the business and the wealth generated.

Capital gain

Capital gain results from selling a capital asset at a higher price than its cost. Whether an investor makes a capital gain depends on the purchase price of an asset compared to its selling price, the effect of depreciation on its value, and whether inflation has bitten into the investor's profit margin.

Capital gains tax

An income tax (gain) arises from changes in asset market value.

Cars

Vehicles provided to employees as part of their compensation.

Cash bonus

A monetary reward given to employees.

Commission

A payment made to employees based on the sales they generate.

Company tax

A tax levied on companies' income, separately from its shareholders' income.

Contributions

Payments made by employees or employers to a plan.

Deferred dividend shares

Shares are issued with the stipulation that shareholders will only be entitled to receive dividends after a specified period, either because the issuing company is incurring losses or because it wants to use the funds for other purposes.

Dividend

A company's profits are usually paid to its shareholders as a yearly (final dividend) or sometimes half-yearly (interim dividend) dividend.

Dividend reinvestment plan

A scheme enabling shareholders in a company to acquire additional shares instead of taking their dividends in cash. For companies, the plans represent a relatively inexpensive source of equity finance. Once a shareholding is registered with a plan, reinvestment occurs automatically each time the company declares a dividend and the shareholder receives a new share certificate.

Dividend yield

The theoretical return on an investment assumes shares are bought on the market at the prevailing price and does not consider charges such as brokerage. It is calculated by dividing the dividend per share by the current share price, expressed as a percentage.

Earnings per share

One of several gauges of a company's performance. It is calculated by dividing the company's earnings by the number of shares on issue to show the profit earned for each share.

Employee ownership

A business model where employees own shares in the company they work for.

Employee share ownership plan

One of a variety of incentive schemes, usually for the benefit of senior executives, is through which a company rewards prized employees by giving them part ownership. This may come in the form of shares paid for by the company, partly paid or contributing shares made available to the employee for a minimal outlay, or options to acquire shares later. Sometimes, the transfer of shares will depend on the employee's promise to stay with the company for a specified time or on achieving a performance target. Where loans from the company finance shares, the shares may be held in a trust, with dividends used to pay off the loans.

Equity

The part of something – asset, house or company –you own. What the professionals call shares. If you lend a company money, you have made a loan and rank as a creditor who, under normal circumstances, would expect repayment of the loan plus interest at a future date. If you buy ordinary shares in a company, you become an equity holder, which means you share in its profits (and losses) and have a less clear-cut idea of your future returns than does a lender. As an ordinary shareholder, you stand in line behind debenture-holders for settlement should the company be wound up. You cannot rely on a fixed return, and you run the risk of loss, but in return for this, you have a share in the company's surplus during good times.

Equity savings plan

A plan that allows employees to save and invest in company shares.

Equity trust

A unit trust that gathers unitholders' funds and invests them in a range of shares through the stock market.

Exit planning

The process of preparing for the transition of ownership or leadership in a company.

Financial incentive

An offer of money is used to induce a performance improvement.

Fringe benefits tax

Employers pay taxes based on the value of fringe benefits provided to employees.

Fully paid shares

Shares on which no uncalled capital is due.

Golden handcuffs

Handsome remuneration is made on the provision that the employee will stay with the company.

Golden hello

A generous upfront payment made by a company to an incoming employee. Like a signing-on fee.

Goods and services tax

An indirect tax is levied as a percentage of the prices for most goods and services.

Incentive

A reward: Employers offer incentives to cultivate loyalty and productivity among workers.

Income tax

Tax levied directly on personal income.

Income continuance policy

A policy that provides income to employees in case of disability or illness.

Investments
Assets acquired with the expectation of generating income or appreciation.

Issue options
The act of granting options to buy shares.

Management buy-out
A transfer of ownership or control of a company to those involved in running the business.

Leveraged buy-out
The company's existing management generally buys a company using borrowed money.

Listed company
A company whose shares are quoted on the stock exchange and are available to be bought and sold by the public.

Long-term (loyalty) bonus
A bonus paid to employees based on their long-term commitment to the company.

Market capitalisation
The stock market assesses a company's value by multiplying the number of shares on issue by the current share price.

Net profit
Gross profit less all expenses such as cost of goods sold, selling expenses, tax and interest on borrowings.

Operating profit/loss
The after-tax profit or loss a business makes from its ordinary revenue-producing activities. Gains and losses derived from activities outside the normal operations of a business are called 'extraordinary items. They are added to or deducted from operating profit to arrive at a 'net profit/loss after extraordinaries'.

Option
A contract that gives the holder, in return for paying a premium to the option seller, the right to buy or sell a financial instrument or commodity during a given period.

Option stocks
Company shares on which options are traded. The Australian Stock Exchange allows options trading on only a limited range of shares.

Ordinary shares
Fully paid shares with voting rights but rank after debentures and preference shares for dividend payments. If the company is wound up, ordinary shareholders rank as unsecured creditors, behind secured creditors such as debenture holders.

Other benefits
Additional perks or advantages provided to employees.

Participating employees
Employees who are eligible to participate in an employee share ownership plan.

Plan Trustee
An individual or organisation responsible for managing a trust or plan.

Profit
The financial gain obtained when revenue exceeds expenses.

Profit-and-loss account
An account showing a company's earnings and expenses over a period, what it has done with its profits, how much is being paid out in dividends and how much is retained in the company.

Purchase options
Financial instruments that give the holder the right to buy shares at a predetermined price.

Redeemable preference shares
Shares that, on a stated maturity date, the issuing company will buy back for face value plus dividend. Being preference shares, they rank ahead of ordinary shares but behind debentures in any claim on the company's assets.

Retained bonus
A bonus that is held back and paid out at a later date.

Revenue
Earnings: what a company makes in monetary terms from its activities. This is not to be confused with profit since expenses must come from revenue.

Salaries and wages
Regular payments made to employees for their work.

Shadow share plan
A plan that provides employees with benefits similar to those of shareholders without actually issuing shares.

Shareholders
Individuals or entities that own shares in a company.

Shareholders' funds
What belongs to the shareholders of a company: issued capital and retained profits.

Shareholders' interest
The net amount of a company's funds that belongs to its shareholders. The shareholders' ratio is calculated by dividing shareholders' funds by the company's total assets.

Shares in company
Units of ownership interest in a company.

Short-term (annual) bonus

A bonus paid to employees based on their performance over a short period, typically a year.

Succession planning

The process of identifying and developing future leaders within a company.

Unit trust

An investment product that enables small investors to pool their funds and earn a greater return than if each investor had acted individually. The investors hold units that may fluctuate in value depending on the market performance of the underlying assets.

Employee Ownership

Dr Craig West

Ask any small or medium-sized business owner what their greatest challenge yet most valuable asset is, and they will all agree – it is their staff. What would it mean to your business if your employees were as committed to achieving success as you are?

With over 25 years of experience as a strategic accountant and adviser to small businesses, Dr Craig West introduces the Peak Performance Trust. This ultimate employee engagement tool will have your high-performing staff think and act less like employees and more like business owners.

The ability to motivate people to peak performance means being able to attract and retain business—and it is a major source of competitive advantage. Can your business afford not to have a Peak Performance Trust?

For more worksheets, articles, advice and information on employee incentive schemes, visit
www.succession.plus.

www.ingramcontent.com/pod-product-compliance
Lightning Source LLC
Chambersburg PA
CBHW040756220326
41597CB00029BB/4955